The Magic of Horses

Horses as Healers

by

Sharon Janus

SunShine Press Publications

SunShine Press Publications, Inc.
PO Box 333
Hygiene, CO 80533

Copyright ©1997 by Sharon Janus

Cover design by James Guzik

Excerpt from "The Horses of Achilles" in
THE COMPLETE POEMS OF CAVAFY copyright © 1961 and renewed 1981 by Rae Dalven
reprinted by permission of Harcourt Brace & Company

Publisher's Cataloging-in-Publication Data

Janus, Sharon.
    The magic of horses : horses as healers / Sharon Janus.
— 1st ed.
      p. cm.
      Includes bibliographical references
      Preassigned LCCN: 97-66587
      ISBN 1-888604-06-9

    1. Horsemanship—Therapeutic use. 2. Recreational therapy.
I. Title

RM931.H6J36 1997   615.8'515
                                     QBI97-40484

Printed in the United States of America
5 4 3 2

Printed on recycled, acid-free paper using soy-based ink

Dedication

For my healers: Netty and Red:
Netty, truly the heart of a Thoroughbred
Red, the patience of seasons
(but mostly Netty)
and
in loving memory of "Z"

Table of Contents

Foreword

This is the first book about horses that has ever taken me to such depths of understanding and appreciation. The author, Sharon Janus, with her no less remarkable skills of observation and empathy than the horses in this work, reveals more about the soul and powers of these animals in these few pages than you will find in most libraries.

In the process of enriching and advancing our understanding of horses, she opens our hearts with the incredible testimonies of the therapeutic benefits horses provide for children and adults. The more evidence that she presents about these physical, emotional, and spiritual benefits as her book unfolds, the more we see the horse through Sharon's eyes: the eyes of the heart. Then like me, you will never see a horse ever again as "just a dumb beast," or as "so much horse flesh." You will see them in a very different light because of her work. It is an enlightened book that gives an enlightening way of seeing and appreciating horses in and for themselves.

As *Black Beauty* showed how brutally horses are treated and continues to move millions of readers to oppose animal abuse, so *THE MAGIC OF HORSES: Horses as Healers* moves us toward a mutually enhancing relationship with animals. This book's testaments to the powers of love open us to the sacred dimension of horses, inspiring us to embrace horses and all of Nature's Creations in reverence and love.

Dr. Michael W. Fox
Veterinarian and Vice President
The Humane Society of the United States
Washington, D.C.

Preface

I hope that this book inspires others, as the stories of the people and their horses have inspired me. May this inspiration be the source of service to others.

Every year 100,000 - 150,000 horses are slaughtered in the United States alone. The world would be a much better place if even one-third of these wonderful animals could be saved, trained, and used to help people in therapeutic riding programs.

Currently in the United States, research into the benefits of therapeutic riding is scanty. No one is sure why riding on horses helps the emotionally and physically challenged, but it does. Often the help is nothing short of miraculous.

When research is done into the therapeutic effects of riding, the reasons for the positive results often remain elusive, evading the best medical and scientific diagnostic equipment and the best trained observers. The explanation is simple: our science can't qualify and quantify everything there is in the world. Some things are by their essence mysterious, miraculous or magic. This is part of the beauty of horses.

All too often, those who suffer from a mental or physical disability are forgotten. Sometimes they are teased, taunted, pitied, ignored or somehow made to feel less than human through the words or actions of others. In reality their accomplishments are awesome, especially their achievements on horseback.

Only those people who ride horses can understand the difficulties and intricacies involved when working with 1,000 pounds of muscle with a mind and strong will all its own.

* * *

Born in 1972, my aged Thoroughbred mare, Sibernet, is responsible for my own experience with a horse's healing power.

My father died when I was five years old, only one month before we were to buy my first pony. The dream of having my very own horse wasn't realized until some 30 years later when Sibernet, or Netty, came into my life and made that dream come true. She's a gorgeous, 16-hand, dark bay, fiery being, and we immediately became best friends. With and because of Netty the promise of a horse of my own was at last fulfilled.

Horse crazy all my life, I naturally spent hours and hours with her, and without really knowing it, she began to fill the void left in my heart by my father's death. Then and still when I look at her, I often feel my father's presence, and deep inside, I know that he never really left. In a strange and mysterious way, she brought me a message, which is that the part of him that I loved so much is in me, though his physical form has returned to his Source.

Not only does Netty fill a void, she has taught me invaluable lessons about living. I often go to the pasture to spend time with her, especially so when I'm feeling harried and off-center. Netty has her two ways of responding to my dark mood. One way is through her businesslike attitude. She clearly communicates the idea that we have work to do, and that we can't be bothered with unnecessary burdens. If she could speak, I'm sure she'd be saying, "Let it go. We've other concerns."

Her other way of responding is to run into the pasture and just stand, either under the sunlight or under the moonlight. She clearly communicates the idea that day to day petty annoyances in life are far less important than the surrounding beauty of nature. At these times, it as if she is telling me that I must learn to let go of all that inhibits my growth as a person. Sometimes her healing magic is dispensed daily.

She has delivered me from harm's way on several occasions, the most notable was when I was caught outside during a raging Colorado snowstorm. I felt that I could no longer go on. I dismounted because the wind was fiercely cold and whipped the snow in both our faces. I was so cold and wet. My pain was nearly unbearable. Netty just arched her neck, faced the wind and trotted on—with me hanging alongside. She kept her pace slow and even, and finally got me safely home, (which just goes to show that animals are kind to dumb people).

Netty is my best friend, my closet and most trusted companion, and my spiritual advisor. I don't believe she is that different from other horses. They all have an inner, uncanny ability to read people and give just what's needed. That is, if we listen well.

Through Netty I've learned that love is gentle and yielding, and that true love is expressed as a desire for the total happiness of the other. Because of her, I'm a better person. I hope I always remain worthy of such pure love and friendship.

Acknowledgments

This book is a gift from those people who tell their stories— without them, it wouldn't be.

I would like to especially thank Nancy Morton at the North American Riding for the Handicapped Association (NARHA) in Denver. Her help was integral to the completion of this task. Thanks to Cindy Sharp and all those people involved who encouraged me to 'Press On,' notably my husband, (who helps make dreams come true) and my son.

Special thanks to my personal long-distance graphic designer, James Guzik. His creativity and hard work is greatly appreciated. Also to Cathie Peterson: these two talented artists are truly world class.

Horses as Healers

Horses are the golden threads with which the fabric of human history has been stitched together. They haunt the pages of world religions, mythologies, and literatures. They've been our symbolic gods, our transportation, our beasts of burden, our companions, our teachers, and sometimes, they've been our healers. As a healer, the horse has a long and rather complex history, a history as old as the story of western civilization.

To the ancient Greeks horses were unlike any other animal in strength, agility, and nobility. Their glorious figures dance atop many ancient structures; their magnificent forms grace vases and pottery of all types and patterns; and famous riders and their mounts speak to us undisturbed from the pages of distant literatures.

One of the most celebrated Greek characters is the centaur Chiron, half man, half horse. According to the scholar Michael Stapleton, Chiron was a storehouse of ancient wisdom and, in fact, the original ancient tribal medicine man.[1] Legend tells us that he gave humanity the great gift of medicine.

Chiron was an expert in the use of medicinal plants and herbs as well as in the art of surgery. He was adept and trusted in prescribing and administering drugs, including parmaka, a deadly poison and toxic killer which was best avoided by all but the most experienced. Dozens of mythological stories celebrate Chiron's impressive healing power. In one story, he performs surgery on a young Achilles whose ankle had been burned through magical practices. Chiron actually replaced Achilles' missing bone with a healthy one taken from a giant's skeleton.[2]

In another story Chiron restored Phoenix's sight, after he was blinded for violating his father's concubine. But not only was Chiron a capable healer, he was also renown for his skills in teaching and instructing others in the medical arts. He tutored the best students in ancient Greece, including his daughter, Ocyrrhoe; Medea's husband, Jason; the great Achilles; and Apollo's son, Asclepius.[3]

So are we to believe in creatures half horse and half human who pranced along the untamed shores of Greece teaching and healing those in need? No, Chiron is a symbol. The ancient Greeks excelled at explaining nature and human nature symbolically.

According to Carl Jung, humans are symbol-making beings. Creating and using symbols is one of our most ancient activities. Religion and art are the domains of the spirit. The human spirit expresses itself symbolically via these two channels, often doing so without the consent of the conscious mind. The symbols that we create are psychologically meaningful and significant to the human spirit.[4]

As a symbol, Chiron represents a being capable of living and moving in two distinct worlds, the animal and the human. Both worlds become one through Chiron's image, much like a horse and rider transform themselves into one entity. He represents the merging of the animal and cultured worlds. Perhaps his ability to blend both worlds is the reason why he had the capacity to heal in the first place.

The Greeks would not have judged this mixture of human and animal odd in any way. They believed that humans could exercise their powers of reason, but could also be quite "beast-like." As far as the ancient Greeks were concerned, humans were most similar to animals. One of the only differences was the fact that through the trappings of civilization, humans are often required to part with their raw or animal side and don the wardrobe and ornaments of a civilized member of society.

As a civilized being in a social setting, humans must balance, ever so gently, the rational and irrational facets in their human nature. It's important to understand that for the classical Greeks neither quality was thought to be better nor worse than the other. It's true, however, that rational thinking in some situations is much better than in others. Like the dark and light side of the moon, each is accepted and acknowledged as one half of a whole.

Chiron remains a potent healing symbol even today. His image graces the veterinary profession. But why was Chiron used by the ancient Greeks as a symbol for healing? Why not another animal, a pig, a goose, or a squirrel? It wasn't accidental that the horse was a symbol for healing power. The ancient Greeks were trying to tell us, through the symbol, that the horse was capable of soothing human troubles.

Chiron's power might have emerged from his mastery of both the human and animal worlds. Or, perhaps his talent derived from his equine empathy. The modern poet Cavafy eloquently suggests that one of the horses' most distinguishing qualities is their unique ability to empathize with humanity. In his poem, *The Horses of*

Achilles, Cavafy explains that Achilles' horses can't stop crying at the sight of his slain friend, Patroclus. Zeus sees the animals weeping and deeply regrets ever having given horses to man:

> *Yet the two*
> *noble animals went on shedding their tears*
> *for the never-ending calamity of death.*[5]

The horses' healing abilities were also highly regarded in other cultures. Native Americans held that the horse was a most powerful instrument in healing for two reasons. One was that horses were considered gifts from the gods, and as gifts, they were naturally imbued with supernatural powers. These powers could be called on to help humans in need. The second reason was that they were able to dwell in both the natural and the supernatural worlds. Given this ability, a horse could intercede or mediate between the divine forces of nature and humanity. With these credentials, it was no wonder horses were regarded and honored as powerful sources of healing.

Plains tribes have similar stories of the horse's creation by either a sky or water deity. They also share a belief that the gods were reluctant to allow humans to have horses on Earth. The gods maintained that humans had a difficult time keeping the Earth and her inhabitants holy. Only after long debate and careful consideration did the gods allow humans the gift of these swift creatures. They then instructed humans on the proper care of horses to ensure the animals' health and prosperity. As humans followed the gods' advice and cared for horses, something wonderful happened—the horse, in turn, cared for humanity. Thus, a sacred bond was forged between the horse and the human.

A result of this bond is the horse's ability to he person's ills. Plains tribes held that all aspects of mental and physical illnesses could be cured by either a live horse or a horse spirit who imparts the necessary knowledge to a person in dreams or in visions.

Even injuries caused by a rebel horse could be set right. An Apache story tells of a man who regains consciousness with the help of the horse who inflicted his nearly fatal injury. The man was roping some wild horses in a corral when the ropes became tangled around his legs. The horse escaped from the enclosure and dragged the man around the dry, rocky landscape until the rope finally snapped. Friends found the man unconscious, bruised, scraped raw, and very nearly dead.

A woman who had horse power, or horse medicine, bestowed on her by a kindly spirit horse, was called while the man was being taken to his tepee. She requested a saddle, bridle, blanket and the offending horse. When these items and the fractious animal had been brought to her, she sang to the injured young man for four days.

On the fourth day, the woman told everyone that the tepee had to be thoroughly cleaned and taken down. The woman then went and untied the horse. The animal went directly to the sick man and rubbed him with his nose, then licked him all over. Next, he went into the trees and pawed in the four sacred directions, north, south, east, and west. Finally, the animal circled the man four times and then ran to catch his herd. At this point, the young man fully recovered.

Horses were said to be invaluable for healing a person's poor mental state, whether its origin was emotional, physical, or spiritual. If someone were listless, had lost his appetite, or suffered from depression, a horse could cure him.

bestowed his medical knowledge on
ed, this person would be summoned to
embers in need. He could also be called
erson injured through a fall, bite, or kick.
it called by the doctor was always the same
offending horse.[6]

Often, these practitioners not only had the powers to heal a person, but could heal a horse as well. An exhausted horse or one with broken bones could be cured by a person with horse medicine. It was even believed that horse medicine could be called on to influence the movements of animal herds, such as buffalo and antelope.[7]

One Apache story describes the origin of horse medicine as a gift from a spirit horse who had the power of speech. The horse befriended an Apache who helped him escape from an enemy tribe. The warrior and the horse lived harmoniously for a time, but the horse soon grew jealous of the warrior's girlfriend. Unable to stand the girlfriend's attentiveness to the warrior, the horse disappeared from the area.

Mourning for his friend, the Apache searched over many mountain ranges finally finding the horse on the fourth range. The animal appeared and told him that he would not return with him. The man cried; the horse pitied him, for he knew then that the warrior loved him. Denying him Earthly companionship, the horse gave him horse medicine power instead.[6]

Horse medicine was frequently exercised as a cure during ceremonies. Many of these ceremonies remain sacred and secret even today. So powerful is this medicine that many Native Americans refuse to speak of it. They believe that used anywhere but in its proper ceremonial context, it can do more harm than good.

One famous horse ceremony took place over several days and is recorded in *Black Elk Speaks*. Black Elk's friend and advisor, Black Road, assisted the medicine man and helped him carry out the Horse Dance in which many tribal members were healed and blessed with spiritual energy.

The Horse Dance reenacts Black Elk's sacred vision. Participants rode black, white, sorrel, and buckskin horses. The four colors corresponded to the four sacred directions. The energy during the ceremony was so overwhelming that the horses danced and pranced on their own, lifting their voices with the members of the tribe as all beings present danced and sang to the four sacred directions.

After the ceremony, Black Elk was surrounded by people who told him that they or their relatives had been healed. Black Elk noted "Even the horses seemed to be healthier and happier after the dance." When the excitement calmed, Black Elk was welcomed into the circle of highly respected and powerful healers.[8]

The Plains Indians' stories and beliefs surrounding the horse as a healer might seem to be based on mere superstitions to many modern readers. Native American medical beliefs and practices have been criticized for their lack of scientific rigor, since they are based on beliefs of the benevolent and malevolent powers within the universe rather than on western scientific methods.

Although it's true that superstitions enter stories, it's equally true that Native Americans lived closer to and better understood nature. Native Americans' knowledge of medicinal herbs and natural remedies was broad. The use of these plants was not casual, but was based on experience and results could be repeated. They approached and dealt with sicknesses and cures with the firm conviction that mind and body profoundly influence one another. This idea has yet to be fully realized by many modern day physicians. Consequently, cures for illnesses are often fragmented and marked by the treatment of symptoms.

It is important to understand that Native Americans wouldn't judge horse accidents and injuries as unusual. First, it's not too hard to fall from a horse—anyone can do it. The Plains Indians believed that a crow feather could help a person remain seated, so many riders wore one as protection. Second, Native Americans were gifted horsemen and horsewomen; they knew of the dangers that resulted from a fall, a kick, or a bite. The dangers were accepted.

Many healing ceremonies were performed because a person was thrown or otherwise injured by a horse. Some Native Americans even believed that broken bones could be healed quickly if the healing ceremony was performed soon after the accident happened.

Is it mere coincidence that horses are held as healers in two cultures so diverse and removed from each other as the ancient Greeks and Native Americans? Or is it possible that horses have powers to heal psychologically, spiritually, emotionally, and physically? Are horses magical in some way? Or are there scientific reasons for their healing abilities which have yet to be discovered?

Today, horses are used successfully as healers. Throughout the United States and Europe, horses are increasingly put to work in therapeutic riding programs. The North American Riding for the Handicapped Association (NARHA) has over 475 centers in 48 states and Canada. NARHA lists the therapeutic benefits of horses as: improving muscle tone, balance, posture, coordination, motor development, and promoting emotional and psychological well-being.

The stories that follow tell of people's experiences with horses and healing. They involve very special people, both able-bodied and physically challenged, and their very special horses. Some people tell of emotional healing; others tell of psychological healing; still others tell of spiritual healing; and some recount stories of physical healing.

Four people tell of serious injuries caused by horses. They then go on to tell of their later healing. Fiona Thomas and Lynn Vannocker have fully recovered from their injuries. Eileen Flickinger and Sandy Dota haven't fully recovered physically. Eileen has made great progress; Sandy has an irreversible spinal injury.

Although none of the four women were ecstatic about their accidents, they all accepted them and moved on with their lives. Most importantly, they all still ride horses and attribute a healing experience to the horse. A dedicated equestrian always gets back in the saddle—no matter what.

The reader will find that many of the following stories are miraculous, and all of them are inspirational. These stories are as diverse as the people who share them with us. Yet these folks have one thing in common: their sensitivity and utter devotion to the animals that have changed their lives, be the change momentary or momentous.

In his book, *Meditations with Animals*, Gerald Hausman writes "In healing, animals give freely of their medicine but only to the deserving."[9] If this statement is true, these people who tell their own stories are certainly "deserving" according to the horses with whom they've shared their lives.

Healing the Head

Gail Claussen
Rush, Colorado

What strikes faster than a rattlesnake? Gail Claussen's wit. Born in Kansas in 1936, there isn't much this old cowboy hasn't done, and he'll willingly share every story lovingly spiced with aphorisms, epigrams, and puns, and generously peppered with wisecracks, satiric quips, and just plain jokes. Imagine a man who combines Mark Twain's humor and John Wayne's brawn, add a voice like thunder, and you got Gail Claussen.

But this crusty old cowboy hasn't always been the picture of happiness. About five years ago, Gail's eyesight started to fail him. A hereditary disorder known as macular degeneration, blood clotting on the retinas, was responsible for the problem, and now Gail is legally blind. His right eye can distinguish between light and dark, and his left eye detects shadows. In order to make out a person's face, Gail says he has to get within four inches, "but the person backs away thinking that I'm trying to kiss him."

It's a stroke of bad luck, to say the least, for a man who owns and operates a 3,000 acre ranch and a herd of 100 Black Angus cattle—cattle descended from livestock that his family has owned since 1929. These animals were originally imported from Scotland.

So how does Gail run his ranch? His beloved wife Karol helps, as do his children, and Silk Shotgun, a seven-year-old, 1,300 pound muscled and heavy registered Quarterhorse stallion. Gail calls him his "seeing-eye horse." Shotgun gets Gail out and about, and rather amazingly, Gail and Shotgun work the cattle together.

"Shotgun heals my head," Gail declares. Shortly after learning of his impending blindness, Gail became very depressed. All that he loved, and all that he did seem threatened. He thought that his ranching days were over, so he sold all but seven animals from his herd. The world was indeed a dark place. In addition to facing major changes in business, he faced changes in his lifestyle. Gail had always led an active life—this man can't sit still. In fact, Gail admits, "I make a nun nervous." The thought of a sedentary life ate at him.

But with the help of family, friends, and Shotgun, Gail's depression lifted. And with time, his Angus herd increased their numbers again.

Shotgun keeps this active cowboy mobile, and he gives Gail the chance to do what he loves, which is to work on the range. Yet it's not a one way street, for Shotgun, too, loves his work. If they need to round up the herd, Gail relies on Shotgun to tell him where the cows can be found. Once the herd is in Shotgun's sight, the horse turns his head in their direction; Gail feels it and knows where to ride. He and Shotgun then go after them.

Gail sees the cattle only as shadows. When they get close, he can distinguish between the cows and the calves—a cow is a big shadow, and a calf is a small shadow. Gail shows Shotgun what needs to be done, and where the cows and calves need to go. Then this well trained horse sets to work, sorting the cows from the calves so that they can be worked through the chutes.

Shotgun is every bit as colorful and as quirky as his handler. A stubborn bull sets his ire ablaze. On two separate occasions, when a neighbor's bull wandered into Gail's pasture, Shotgun turned matador. Both times, Gail was able to safely ride out Shotgun's angry display. The first time, Shotgun bit the bull's neck, thumped him on the head with his forelegs, then whirled around and kicked him in the belly with his hind legs. The bull got the idea and went home. The second time, a twilight evening, Shotgun bit the bull on the back and chased him home.

When Shotgun isn't working, he's quite the stallion. All the mares admire his brains and brawn, and Gail says that "he'll chase a horse trailer a mile because he knows that his date's inside." Shotgun's moonlighting even "buys the hay for all the horses."

When Gail's riding, Shotgun is all business and can even be ridden next to a mare in season. Gail rides in the pastures and on the roads of the ranch he loves and knows so well. His trust in Shotgun is unlimited.

Although Gail's blindness has slowed his pace, he still works his cattle and checks and repairs his own fences by riding alongside and running a hammer on the wire. If he finds a break, he fixes it. Gail says that he's still trying to find someone to hold his nails while he drives them, but so far, he hasn't had much luck there.

If Gail isn't around the ranch, there's a good chance he'll be talking and laughing with his friends at the Rush Cafe, a local hangout. Here he kicks up his heels and sharpens his wit with his neighbors, who are "great folks."

Gail is rich in love and friendships. His wife, family, neighbors, and friends mean everything to him. He says that at times, he gets sick and tired of the inconvenience caused by his blindness, but when sadness threatens Gail, he drives it away with the help of his family, friends, and seeing-eye stallion.

This cowboy tells it straight: "The outside of a horse is good for the inside of a man."

Healing Self-Reliance

Sandy Dota
Bangor, Pennsylvania

One chilly November morning in 1980, Sandy Dota was enjoying a trail ride, a ride that would change her life forever. As she rounded a bend, a large dog lunged at her horse. The horse spooked, reared and threw Sandy onto the ground. Looking at her legs, Sandy saw that "they were lying twisted on each other." She tried to straighten them out but couldn't. The agonizing pain in her back, along with her inability to move her legs, told Sandy that the injury was serious.

Her horse ran back to the barn, as Sandy held onto the dog for comfort and warmth. Forty minutes later, she was found and immediately taken to the hospital. Her back was broken, her spinal cord injured, and she was paralyzed from the waist down.

For a time after the injury, Sandy was a recluse. She admits that "I didn't care to go anywhere." Even shopping was off limits because she didn't like the way people stared at her since it made her feel ill at ease. She felt herself no longer a shopper, but an obstacle—big and clumsy in her wheelchair.

Sandy credits a beautiful mare named Brandy for her healing, spectacular comeback, and subsequent riding successes. She was the first horse Sandy rode after her accident in 1980. "My own horse put me in this chair," Sandy notes, "Brandy took me out." Brandy was Sandy's inspiration and motivation, as well as a disciplinarian and a teacher.

"Brandy," Sandy explains, "expected more of me. Walking and trotting weren't enough. Brandy taught me to trust her. Once trust was established, she taught me more. She was always totally tuned into my body and its needs. She ignored my distracting legs as they flopped and banged at her sides, all the while encouraging me to use my upper body for control and balance. Brandy taught me things and made me do things I never thought possible."

Today, people still stare at Sandy, but not because she's in a wheelchair. They stare at the beauty and grace of Sandy and her 1,200 pound Quarterhorse, Bo Diddley. When they practice or demonstrate the classical art of Dressage all eyes are on them.

After watching Sandy and Bo's performance in 1993, one newspaper writer commented: "To watch Ms. Dota ride atop her Quarterhorse is somewhat akin to viewing a dance."

Sandy's and Bo's elegant and seemingly effortless dance movements didn't just appear overnight. Though she was back in the saddle ten months after the accident, she needed lots of support. One person led the horse and two others walked alongside. Through her persistence and hard work, she became an independent rider once again—and what an independent rider she became.

Sandy has won over 50 first-place ribbons in various competitions.

In 1985, she competed on the national level for disabled equestrians and won the New Jersey Governor's Trophy for Horse Person of the Year. The previous year, the honor was presented to the United States Olympic Equestrian Team. In 1988, Sandy was reserve champion at the Sussex County Horse Show sanctioned by the American Driving Society in New Jersey; yes, Sandy also drives. In 1991, Sandy represented the United States in the Second World Dressage Championships for Disabled Riders in Vilhelmsborg, Denmark. She placed fifth out of the 100 riders representing 18 countries. She took second in her disability, nonambulatory paralysis. Her list of honors goes on and on.

Sandy and Bo trained using the French method of Dressage, Riding in Lightness. Bo responds to the slightest of slight touches. Under the guidance of her trainer, Monsieur Racinet, Sandy and Bo performed lateral work, flying lead changes, passage and piaffe—without the use of her legs. As far as anyone knows, Sandy is the first and only nonambulatory rider to realize such feats—feats, it must be added that many able-bodied riders only dream of accomplishing.

Brandy was a very special horse in Sandy's life; Bo Diddley is yet another. Others think so too, since Bo Diddley was actually the model for the 1996 Breyer Therapy Model, Little Andy Wind.

Sandy and Bo don't compete much anymore. Sandy's simply too busy. She is a past vice president of the North American Handicapped Riding Association (NARHA) and often takes part in their training programs to certify riding instructors. Sandy, herself, is a certified therapeutic instructor. Sandy is also certified with the American Judging Association and is often called on to judge at shows. She is a member of the United States

Cerebral Palsy Athletic Association (USCPAA) and the Committee for Standards & Guidelines for International Competition for Equestrian Sports. She is a member of the International Paralympic Equestrian Committee, and she served on the 1996 Team USA Paralympic Equestrian Selection Committee. In addition, she has and continues to present papers on competition and judging guidelines for disabled riders throughout the United States and Canada. Sandy is also a wife and mother.

The poet, Henry Taylor, said that to ride a horse, you must "keep one leg on one side, the other leg on the other side, and your mind in the middle." Taylor suggests that riding is accomplished with the mind, not necessarily the body. Sandy shows that riding is an activity of the mind, as well as of the human spirit.

The Healing Touch

The Carousel
Colorado Springs, Colorado

The Carousel, a therapeutic riding center open since 1990, is dedicated to making small miracles happen for the children it serves. Lisa Keller, who operates The Carousel, states "Our special students encourage us everyday with their bright smiles and bold self-esteem." Two children in particular have encouraged, as well as inspired all of the riding instructors.

One frail, small seven-year-old boy has been riding for two years; he has cerebral palsy, a brain shunt, and hip replacements. When he was first assessed for enrollment, he showed no signs of any emotions, nor any signs of a desire to talk with others.

Over the initial course of six weeks, he never displayed any emotions. A back rider, sitting behind him, was needed to ensure his safety and to manipulate his arms and legs in an effort to promote muscle relaxation. The rider also had to hold up the child's head, since it flopped down onto his chest.

One day, the back rider told the boy, "If you want me to hold your head up, then say 'Up'." Slowly, his ice blue eyes met with hers and he said "Up." Everyone present was elated. It was a small step, but it was a step nonetheless. "It was a little miracle," said Lisa.

The other child, a five-year-old girl, had recently been adopted by loving parents who sought help for the emotionally torn and nonresponsive victim of abuse. Lisa saw her as a needy child who had "retreated into a shell. She trusted no one—especially 'big people.' She showed no emotions or even facial expressions."

Lisa was very careful about choosing a horse for the child; she had to prove to the little girl that there is good in life. For five weeks, she took her riding lessons. She was emotionless and totally detached from everything around her.

At the end of the sixth week, Lisa witnessed a breakthrough. The girl bent down and whispered something into the horse's ear.

During the seventh session, the little girl and the horse were led to the arena. Lisa held out her hand for the child to take, and she did. All observers fought back their tears as she took her first step toward healing.

Helping miracles happen is The Carousel's mission. The Carousel is proof that good things do sometimes come wrapped in small packages.

Healing Gaits

Robin and Joyce Ryan
Longmont, Colorado

Robin Ryan was born with agenesis of the tibia, a short femur bone and no tibia or shin bone. After many surgeries to prepare her for a prosthesis, Robin was fitted. Soon after, she developed scoliosis, curvature of the spine.

Robin wore a body brace 12 hours a day for almost three years. The doctors told Robin's mom, Joyce, that her little girl might never walk, and if by some chance she did, it wouldn't be for long.

When Robin turned four, her physical therapist suggested therapeutic riding. Both Robin and Joyce embraced the idea. Robin immediately liked riding, and Joyce remembers her daughter's first day: "Robin sat so straight you'd have thought that she was an old cowhand." Robin immediately liked riding and now at age 13, continues to ride not only because it helps her physically but because of her love for horses. Robin says, "I love horses. They are so graceful—I love that."

Indeed riding has helped Robin tremendously. In fact, the scoliosis hasn't progressed, but it has been arrested. Her body strength, balance, coordination, and flexibility have all improved, as has her self-esteem.

The booster shot of self-esteem that the horses give Robin is much appreciated, especially in the face of the unabashed cruelty of others. One such incident happened when Robin was eight months old and in a body cast from a recent surgery. Joyce took her to the grocery store when a woman sarcastically, and quite rudely, asked Joyce if she had dropped her baby.

But Robin is one tough horse person, and to prove it, she has a wall in her room decorated with the ribbons she has won in local horse shows. She takes part in all aspects of the horse's care, including grooming, saddling, and feeding. When she gets older, Robin wants to be a veterinarian—horses only.

Robin has astounded her doctors with her progress, just as she impresses others when she's on a horse in the ring. She rides either a gray Arabian named Tar, or a chestnut mare named Pippy.

Joyce describes Robin as a happy person. And when she's on a horse, her happiness only increases. This whirlwind can't be left alone at the stables. Joyce says, "She'll go galloping off on one of her favorite horses with her best friend, Jessica, at her side." At these times, Robin's shining spirit and sweet smile intensify, radiating warmth and contentment to all lucky enough to share in her life.

Healing a Nation

Ery Broman
Espoo, Finland

In Ery Broman's native Finland, horses are most special animals for having saved the country from ruin.

Finland declared its independence from the Soviet Union in 1917, but with the outbreak of World War II, Finland's independence was again threatened. When the Soviets attacked Finland in 1939, the Finnish were outraged. They were not about to give up what they had fought so hard to reclaim. In 1941, after yet another attack, Finland challenged the Soviet Union.

Approximately 1/66th the size of the Soviet Union, and with one Finnish soldier to every 17 Soviet soldiers, Finland beat its enemy, won its land, and recovered its cherished independence.

The hardy Finnish Horse was their secret weapon. Harsh conditions that winter made it impossible to use even moderate sized vehicles in the war effort. Trucks were simply unable to move in the 6 1/2 feet of snow that blanketed the eastern frontier where the Soviets landed. Moreover, even if fuel had been available, the Finnish trucks would not start in the 40 degrees below zero temperature.

With the exception of the best stallions and mares, all the available Finnish horses were called to serve their country, and all farmers willingly volunteered their horses. Each farmer was given a receipt for each horse, and each horse was identified by a number and was transported to the eastern frontier by railway.

The light draft Finnish horse stands 15.2 hands high. These plucky animals are very tough and surefooted. Of the 62,168 animals called to serve their country, 48,573 returned.

The horses pulled the army's canons to the rocky eastern war zone, delivered messages back and forth to the front, carried the dead and dying, and delivered food to the men on the firing lines. Any Finlander will tell you, as Ery Broman readily admits, "Without the horses, the country would have been lost."

The horses not only withstood the rocky terrain, the frigid temperatures, and the 6 1/2 feet of snow, they also empathized with the Finlanders. Many somehow seemed to know what was at stake. In one account, a war veteran reports his horse saved him from enemy hands. On his way from the front lines to distribute communications, his horse stopped and would go no further. In fact, the horse didn't move during the entire night. Finally, at the break of dawn, the horse carried him through the forest to where his comrades were waiting. He was informed that earlier that morning Soviets had been captured near the camp.

Not only did the horses empathize with the nation's cause, they exercised uncanny intelligence. The Soviets had aircraft, but the Finnish didn't. When the Finnish horses heard the Soviet planes, most went down to the ground, remaining still, as if not to be sighted. Even after the war, some horses still went down when they heard the sound of nearby aircraft. This often caused commotion in the harried streets of Finnish towns as buses waited until the horses got up and walked off the street.

Most of the Finlanders did not mind the minor inconvenience, for the horses healed the country. They restored the nation's pride and patriotism, its sense of safety and identity, and, perhaps most important, its honor.

Just as the Finnish horses were carried east to the war by the railway, they also returned home by railway. It's said that many of the animals knew their handlers upon their return. It's also said that the veteran horses were reluctant to ever travel east again.

Ery Broman's grandfather, Arne Grahn, volunteered six horses to the war effort. Only one mare returned home to the family. She was immediately retired, as were most equine veterans. Whenever Ery travels to the United States a piece of her homeland accompanies her. She carries a lock of hair from this mare's mane as a reminder of her country, her past, and her future.

Healing the Mind

Ceci Flanagan
New Brunswick, Canada

When Ceci Flanagan found herself getting divorced and without a job, she didn't worry. She knew that she could support herself and her five-year-old son, David. For even though she lacked experience, she had two college degrees. But Ceci had no idea how she'd ever be able to support her horse, Ranger, a bay Standardbred. "The thought of losing him," Ceci says, "was unbearable. It was worse than the death of my marriage."

Reluctantly, she approached Michael Phelan, the owner of the stable where Ranger was boarded. She explained her situation to him. With a heavy heart, Ceci asked Michael to help her sell Ranger.

Michael felt her sadness over selling Ranger and he suggested an alternative. In exchange for room and board for David, Ranger, and herself, Ceci mucked, fed, and cared for the 35 horses at the stable.

"It was a terrible year mentally, but the horses got me through it," she explains, "especially Ranger. He eased my pain by just being there and listening to me." Ceci told him all of her problems, cried into his thick mane and hung around his neck. Sometimes Ranger just listened; sometimes he'd nuzzle her to let her know that she was loved and needed. Whenever she had to talk or cry, Ceci went to Ranger's stall.

David, too, spent much time in Ranger's stall. Armed with dinky little toys, he'd build imaginary roads in the bedding, playing beneath Ranger's feet for hours. Ranger never moved, but Ceci believes he was relieved when David had to go eat dinner or get ready for bed.

As in most well run stables, routine was of the utmost importance. Ceci's day began early; she fed and mucked, then let the horses out. On most days, after the work was done, she'd go watch the horses graze. Perched on the highest point of the property, the manure pile, Ceci drank tea and stared at the horses, oblivious to all else. Her mind went blank, allowing her time to simply be, to be herself, to be silent and to exist for a time without emotional or financial troubles gnawing away at her.

After a year of silently watching the horses graze, and of telling her problems and concerns to Ranger, Ceci was healed. She could return to the world. A world where David was ready to begin school.

Shortly after leaving her job at Michael's stable, Ceci met a wonderful man. Dan and Ceci have been married for over 15 years. David has grown and moved on to his own life in Vancouver.

Ceci now operates a successful public relations firm and has aquired her Level I Coaching Certificate from the Canadian Equestrian Federation. This allows her to teach others the joys and art of horsewomanship.

Sadly, Ranger is no longer with Ceci, but he remains forever in her heart. She admits, "Ranger kept me sane. He patiently taught me to grow as you go."

Ceci's new horse, Finnigan's Rainbow, is an 18-hand Hanoverian Thoroughbred cross. "He has that same wonderful, soft, kind eye and loving personality. But unlike Ranger, Finnigan gets to share in much happier conversations."

Healing Hands

Ravenswood Equestrian Center
Bismarck, Arkansas

If angels or other benevolent beings live and move among human mortals, Judy Fletcher is one of them. Judy has been helping the handicapped regain control over their lives since 1968. She has helped hundreds of students—her youngest was four, her oldest was 80. She works with both the mentally and physically challenged, and she has trained close to a hundred or so therapeutic riding instructors from all over the United States. Much to Judy's delight, she has made hundreds of friends during her 26 years of practicing healing through therapeutic riding.

It all began in Chicago where, as a teenager, Judy was a riding instructor. A woman asked whether or not Judy could help her daughter ride a horse. Even though the child had cerebral palsy, "it would mean the world to her."

Judy quickly agreed to help. When she first met the little girl, the child couldn't sit up, nor could she hold her head up, and since she lacked control over her neck muscles, she couldn't even swallow. After two years of riding, the girl had gained enough muscular control to actually sit on a horse without someone supporting her, and she could even swallow.

Shortly after this success, Judy moved to Arkansas where she owns and operates Ravenswood Equestrian Center. She describes this nonprofit organization as an "asylum for the terminally horsey. The school's colors are black and blue."

Judy certainly believes in the healing power of horses. She has always drawn upon the Shamanistic traditions of healing to help achieve success. It seems that there is no limit to Judy's energy; her day begins at 5:30 in the morning and ends at 11:00 at night. There is no problem Judy won't tackle.

A few years back, a little boy who had been born without arms sought the help of Judy and Ravenswood. He wanted to learn how to ride a horse, and even though his condition posed a problem, Judy and her team of young volunteers soon came up with a solution. One girl suggested using a snorkeling tube to lengthen the reins. So after cutting and fitting the tube and its mouthpiece, the little boy was able to hold the reins in his mouth, and, yes, he learned to ride.

Still another situation that some people might think impossible is Judy's teaching blind children to ride while the horses jump. "They don't need to see," Judy notes. "The horses can see. The children have to be able to count the horse's strides. So the children counted, and the horses jumped—on a lunge in a round pen—the horses and riders jumped."

Judy's successes are truly phenomenal, but she has a lot of help in reaching her outstanding achievements and nearly impossible goals. First, are the "girls." A group of 9-15 year-old adolescents who donate their time to help care for the horses, raise the needed funds, and work with the people who seek Judy's help. The girls also show Judy's Appaloosa horses, and are a world-class equestrian team. Second, Judy has the Arkansas Appaloosa Club. "They are all wonderful people and they're fun to show with," Judy states. Finally, Judy has her horses—who are ever so special.

Judy's Appaloosa horses, Love and Princess, have qualified for world championships at least three times, and all of Judy's horses are cross-trained. They can jump, barrel race, compete in trail classes, and rein.

Besides their cross-training, each horse used for the therapeutic program has more than two years of special training. The horses are trained to distinguish between a rider's cues versus a rider's muscle tremors. They're trained to sense fear, and help the rider overcome it. Most importantly, they're trained to freeze if a rider happens to suffer a seizure during a session.

One student who has made remarkable progress at Ravenswood is Will. Now 11 years old, Will has cerebral palsy. When he first met Judy, he walked, but it was labored. After two years of riding, however, Will is mobile. Judy describes him as "Mr. Personality."

Another student who has made astounding progress is Keach, who suffered a severe head injury in a car accident. Keach was told that he'd never walk again, but he does with the help of a cane. "What's most astounding about Keach," Judy says, "is that he is a remarkable athlete. He had the disabled riders trail class in the bag for 1996." Judy also describes Keach as "a real champion."

Judy, too, is a real champion at what she does. She describes herself as a farmer at heart, a person who likes to watch things grow, and she believes that she'll answer for what she does in this life. If this is true, her million-acre Appaloosa horse ranch in the next world awaits—and its crop will be love.

Healing the Body

Cheri Boyd
Bismarck, Arkansas

During the last polio epidemic to hit New Orleans in 1955, Cheri Boyd contracted the disease. She was only two months old at the time and her parents, a registered nurse and a doctor, had taken all the precautions to keep her safe.

Now, Cheri suffers from postpolio syndrome. Overtaxing her good muscles throughout the years has resulted in their overall weakening. It is as if the good muscles have doubled their age from overuse. Cheri's left thigh muscle, right calf muscle, and feet are affected the most. Sometimes, if she stands for too long a stretch, her legs just give out.

Climbing stairs is a big challenge for Cheri. She has to pick up her left leg and put it down on each step. Her illness, however, has not affected her love for horses. She says that she was never afraid of them and has always admired them. She admired them so much that she started riding seriously six years ago.

Solely because of riding, Cheri's back muscles have strengthened, allowing her to walk further. Her limp has also lessened. Cheri says, "learning to keep my weight on my backside when a horse moves has helped build my upper and lower body strength." The low center of gravity required for staying in the saddle has helped Cheri's overall balance as well. Cueing with her legs has helped to strengthen these muscles where it is especially needed. It can, however, still be a challenge with her weak left thigh.

Accepting challenges is Cheri's hobby. Her doctors were concerned about her carrying a child to full term. Yet, Cheri gave birth to Bob and Chris, now young adults.

Riding in the winter is yet another challenge, since temperatures below 45 degrees Fahrenheit cause Cheri's muscles to cramp. Still, she takes her 13-year-old chestnut Quarterhorse, Hot Shot, out on the trails, although not as often as in spring and summer.

Cheri is an expert rider. Judy Fletcher, her friend and riding instructor, states that "Cheri could ride a horse up a tree and has." Cheri says, "My illness sometimes makes me feel like I'm eighty years old."

"When Cheri turns eighty," Judy quips, "she'll still be riding a horse up a tree."

Healing Mind, Body, and Spirit

Karen Green
Hot Springs, Arkansas

Karen Green was diagnosed with multiple sclerosis in 1991. Needless to say, the news was shocking to Karen and her family. She had always been very active. For years she traveled the country as a representative for a well-known cosmetic company.

Karen rode horses before her illness, but after learning about her condition, she deliberately sought the help of four-legged therapists by enrolling at the Ravenswood Equestrian Center in 1994. She says, "I heard that riding was good for people with disabilities."

Judy Fletcher paired Karen with Love. Karen says, "Love is a fantastic horse. In fact, all of Judy's horses are well trained."

Riding restores Karen's confidence, and also gives her a great sense of success. "I can't walk," she says, "but when I'm on a horse, I can walk a long way. Even though I don't have feeling on my left side, I can still get the horse to respond." This sense of accomplishment is most fulfilling for Karen.

Love not only provides Karen with a feeling of achievement, but riding helps her physically as well. Judy says that through riding, Karen has gained strength. Karen agrees, stating that "The good muscles have strengthened, and since the multiple sclerosis has affected my memory, Love stimulates my brain because riding forces a person to concentrate."

Karen tries to get others involved in therapeutic riding. When she goes to her water therapy, she asks her friends to join in at Ravenswood. To alleviate any possible fears they may have, Karen informs her friends that, "Horses sense when you have a problem, and they compensate for you." Karen trusts Love completely, and believes that the emotional bond they share is every bit as strong as the physical bond. "I rely on Love," she states.

Karen has competed in the Arkansas Appaloosa Club's trail class. During the competition, Karen learned that she could keep up with any able-bodied person. She laughs and says, "Some of the able-bodied didn't do half as well as I did."

Recently, Karen bought a strawberry Appaloosa mare named Chocolate Showers, or just Miss Showers. She is a 16-hand 1,000 pound mare. According to Judy, "the mare follows Karen around like a puppy dog." The mare is gentle but powerful—much like Karen. Judy often describes Karen to others as "a pixie on steroids," since Karen is a petite woman but a "real power house." In essence, Karen is known by her friends as a tenacious woman who does things full board.

Despite her disability, Karen's life is quite busy. She has a husband, two children, and one grandchild, plus her weekly riding sessions with Judy and Miss Showers.

But no matter how busy life gets, Karen admits that she has learned "to stop and smell the roses."

Healing An Athlete

Keach Finley
Hot Springs, Arkansas

Keach Finley had always led an active, athletic life, even working as a cowboy on a Quarterhorse ranch in Texas. Then in March 1993 when Keach was 17 years-old, he was in a nearly fatal car accident in Sandy Creek, Texas. When the police found him, they called an ambulance, even though they thought it too late.

The ambulance attendants revived him, but Keach had suffered a head injury which left him in a coma for five months and in traditional rehabilitation for another six months. Keach was told he'd never walk again. Even though he had been wearing his seat belt and had stayed in the car, the sudden stop of the vehicle crashing into a tree while traveling at 115 mph had caused severe trauma to his brain.

In 1994, not long after his release from the rehabilitation center, Keach sought the help of Ravenswood and Judy Fletcher.

He returned to riding after the accident as he had always liked horses—natural for Keach. By April 1995, he was jumping the horse, although he preferred the trail classes.

He loves Judy's Appaloosas, stating, "These horses have a lot of brains. They're easy to work with."

At Ravenswood, he rides Princess and says that she has helped him in many ways. His coordination has improved, and he's learning to use his left hip in place of his foot to signal Princess. "Most noteworthy," Keach says, "Princess has helped me to walk better, and she has made me a bit more friendly."

It's hard to imagine Keach could be any more friendly. Judy reports that after every performance at the Arkansas Appaloosa Shows, "Keach gets a standing ovation. He's so personable that everyone loves him." Judy adds, "He's a tremendous athlete, a true champion who works very hard to succeed."

A true champion indeed. Keach has held the title of Reserve Champion since 1995. Judy states that he is harder on himself than is anyone else, and he'll do what he has to until it's right, for he accepts nothing less than perfection.

"Keach was already walking when he came to Ravenswood," Judy says, "but riding has made him even more mobile." The injury still affects Keach's motor control on his left side and his right eye, but his progress is truly miraculous. Keach is living proof that it's unwise to underestimate the will of a champion.

Healing Rhythms

Janet and Will Stevens
Murfreesboro, Arkansas

Will Stevens was born with cerebral palsy. His pediatricians wondered if he would ever be able to make much developmental progress. At the age of six, he had surgery on the sensory nerves at the base of his spinal column to lessen his spasticity. With the help of much traditional therapy, Will learned to walk.

His pediatricians encouraged Janet, Will's mom, to seek out and use other forms of therapy. While talking to her parents on the phone in Friendship, Arkansas, Janet expressed her desire to somehow find a therapeutic riding program. Soon afterwards, Janet's parents saw a newspaper featuring an article on Judy Fletcher and Ravenswood Equestrian Center. Janet remembers, "The answer to my prayer came in a mysterious way."

Will began taking riding lessons at Ravenswood where Judy has helped with his progress. Janet says, "Judy wanted Will to gain strength. No one just sits on a horse at Ravenswood. Judy has him trail riding, reversing through L-shaped partitions, making figure eights, circles, opening and closing gates, dog legs—you name it, he does it." At first, Judy sat behind Will when he rode. Then he progressed to riding alone with sidewalkers.

Traditional therapy has been enhanced by Will's therapeutic riding. Both Janet and Will's doctor see dramatic improvements because of the horses. When he first started riding, he was walking with braces and a walker and it was labored. Now Will is using crutches during his more traditional therapy sessions. Will's balance, flexibility and coordination have really improved since he began riding. "Even his physical therapist sees a difference," Janet reports. In addition, Will's self-concept has greatly benefitted. When he's on a horse, he can compete with anybody—even an able-bodied person. "When Will talks horses," Janet adds, "he beams."

When Will began riding at Ravenswood, he rode Love. Eventually he competed with her in the show ring. Will placed first in the disabled riders trail class in 1994, and has four trophies to commemorate his riding accomplishments.

Will now has his own horse, a 16 hand, chestnut gelding named Socks. Socks lived at Ravenswood until he developed a heart murmur; he then moved to Will's house. Will's entire family—mom, dad, and brother Rob—agree, "Socks has us well trained. We're an obedient bunch."

Will usually rides Socks on Friday afternoons in any and all kinds of weather. But he's certainly missed around Ravenswood. Judy states, "Will is the most personable kid that I've ever met. If he has a problem, he just works around it." Everyone at Ravenswood agrees that Will is one of the most lovable characters that they've ever known.

When asked what he thinks about horses, Will responded: "Horse riding is so much fun. I like all parts of it. I especially like the training and competing." The beam in Will's eye is proof that he enjoys every second spent with a horse.

Healing the Right Side

Eileen Flickinger
Hamburg, Pennsylvania

Eileen Flickinger was riding ponies when she was five years old. As she got older, she progressed to horses and jumping competitions. By the time she was 21, Eileen was quite an accomplished horsewoman. Then in 1982, just two weeks shy of her 29th birthday, tragedy struck. Eileen's horse ran into a fence during a show. Though she was wearing the required hard hat, no safety harness was required at the time. Her hunt cap flew off before she hit the ground, and Eileen suffered an injury to her brain stem leaving her in a coma for three months.

Amazingly, Eileen came out of the coma, but more amazing still is that one week before her 30th birthday, Eileen was already back in the saddle. Her occupational therapist had encouraged her to get back to riding. Eileen welcomed this idea as horses were, and still are, her passion.

When Eileen first returned to her passion, her spasticity limited her to summer riding. She was advised to ride all year long, even though the spasticity is more pronounced in the winter months.

Eileen's father, John, said that progress in physical therapy was reflected in riding, and progress in riding was reflected in physical therapy. Eileen has made truly amazing progress.

Eileen's fall left her a right hemiplegic, meaning she lost all use of the right side of her body. "It's a severe handicap if you're a right-handed person," Eileen notes. "Try dressing yourself with your left hand." But with her courage, persistence, and stubbornness, she taught herself how to write with her left hand, and with the help of horses, she went from a wheelchair to a four-point cane, to a smaller based quad cane, and finally to a single point cane, which she "doesn't always use around the house."

For a time after her accident, Eileen coped with her immobility. "Then after awhile, I got itchy. I wanted to move," she says. So she moved—all the way to the stables.

When she first got on a horse one year after her near tragedy, Eileen had five people helping: one person led, one sat behind her, two walked alongside, and one walked behind. Today, she rides alone, and she's back to participating in horse shows. Several of the shows are sponsored by USCPAA, NARHA, and ASPIRE. These groups encourage mentally and physically challenged people to participate in athletic events, many of which are international.

In 1995, during a competition camp for those long-listed for the 1996 Paralympics, Eileen was thrown. She called it "an unauthorized, unassisted, flying dismount." It left her lying on the ground, soon to be surrounded by police, firemen, EMT's and others. Naturally everyone had rushed to find out how she was. But, anyone could tell that she was a true equestrian, for as the judge approached, Eileen asked, "Up 'till now, how did I do?"

The EMT's just shook their heads. The experience could have scared any other person away from horses forever, but Eileen endured. Her attitude is strong as stone. "When things get hard," she says, "I remember the name of a horse I knew in my junior days, 'Press On, Regardless'." Eileen takes her cue from him and like any athlete, she presses on.

Her unyielding philosophy seems inherited from her father, John, who notes that after Eileen's accident, "The family never looked back. We looked ahead, just like a person is told to do when she is first learning to horseback ride."

Over the years, many equine therapists have helped Eileen regain both her self-esteem and her sense of physical well-being. For through riding, Eileen has regained her balance and mobility. Each week she rides a different horse, unless she's preparing for a show. Currently, Eileen is working with Dapples, an aged 15.1-hand dapple-gray Thoroughbred mare. She believes, "The horse is a therapist."

Horses keep Eileen busy, but she still finds time to sew; her specialties are patchwork and applique, and it's no surprise that horses are featured on each item. Eileen proudly adds, "I'm a state-juried member of the Pennsylvania Guild of Craftsmen." Eileen admits, "Nothing will keep me down."

Quoting the poet, Robert Frost, she smiles and softly adds, "I have 'miles to go before I sleep.' "

Healing Through Healing

Pam Bradford
Parker, Colorado

A horse in the garage? Well, he had a serious leg injury and needed constant attention and the garage was the closest building to the house. A turkey in the bathtub? Well, he had a respiratory problem and required steam treatments along with daily doses of nose drops. These and many more sights are commonplace at Pam Bradford's home. Pam has devoted her entire life to helping animals; she rescues, nurtures, loves, and heals the animals in need who come into her life. But she has a most special place in her heart for horses. She's certifiably horse crazy, and readily confesses that horses are her obsession.

Pam got her first pony when she was four years old and has had horses ever since. Pam's mom, Bulah, made certain that her children would always have their animals near them. Much like bread and milk, animals were a staple in the household. Love of and devotion to animals courses through Pam's blood. Her family history suggests it's genetic: Pam's grandmother was a Native American;

Pam's grandfather was an Irishman. Both cultures value horses.

Some of the animals that Pam has healed live with her while others have been placed in safe homes. Pam doesn't discriminate. If an animal—any animal—needs help, they get it. One Christmas Eve several years back, Pam came upon a dog that had been hit by a car. She knew the animal was in shock and quickly called all of the veterinarians in the area. The only vet she could get to help was Dr. Sandy Eckles of Cottage Veterinary located in the center of town. Pam left Sandy's clinic at 10:30 p.m. certain and relieved that the dog was in good hands and would make it.

In some cases it's Pam's own animals that need help. Zeena, a Quarterhorse Appaloosa cross, was born in May 1996. During birth, she suffered an injury to her tongue nearly tearing it in half. Only after months of loving care did she fully recover, and it was a long and expensive road to recovery.

Zeena spent some time in the animal hospital, and according to one vet, it didn't look like she would make it. But she did and returned home, with her face wrapped in gauze from her eyes to her muzzle. The bandages held tubes in place—tube feeding kept her alive.

Zeena also had to be force-fed formula for a time. Against the odds, the filly learned to nurse without using her tongue, until her mother developed a raging infection in her teats. It was one crisis after another for poor Zeena—and for poor Pam. Months later, at home and doing well, Zeena still couldn't go outside to play, since her tongue hung from her mouth and would get sunburnt. Through Pam's patience and loving care, Zeena is now fully recovered, and, yes, her tongue is entirely in her mouth. "Zeena is arrogant and brimming with self-confidence," Pam adds proudly.

Zero, Zeena's mother, came from a home where she was abused and neglected. She was malnourished when Pam got her and had a horrible eye injury. This injury needed reconstructive surgery.

Pam also rescued Trevor, a 16-hand, 2,200 pound Belgian gelding, from a testing laboratory. When he arrived at Pam's house, he couldn't be stabled as he was terrified of what might happen to him. He became unruly when confined to small areas. He could not even find comfort in a corral, since it terrified him just as much as a stall. Nevertheless, Pam worked with Trevor. To make him comfortable, she allowed him access to the pasture at all times.

After months of tender loving care, the giant showed he could in fact trust humans again. Trevor came around. He and Pam are now best friends, and he loves to be ridden by his trusted companion.

Pam gives a lot of care, concern, and love to her patients, but she gets much in return as the healing is reciprocal. Pam heals the animals' emotional or physical ills, and they help heal her spirit and emotions through their priceless gifts of joy and love. They are Pam's sole source of relief from stress. "If things aren't going well," she says, "thirty minutes in the barn is all I need and all's well once again."

Just being near her horses is healing. Pam believes that horses are very spiritual and mystical animals. Perhaps these two qualities are the root of her obsession.

Pam's leisure hours are spent with her horses as are her working hours. She works with polo ponies and runs a pet sitting service. Pam recently opened an equine related insurance agency, named the E.K. Group.

She has been a commercial insurance underwriter since 1977 and decided to branch off on her own. This allows her more time to spend with her horses.

Clearly, Pam's life would be empty without her furred companions. She says that her animals are her family. To some people money is important, to others prestige, but to Pam the most important thing in life is self-satisfaction. She finds this in and through her furry and feathered friends. Pam explains that her life is rich in experiences and satisfaction. Because of her animals, she receives daily doses of this fulfilling tonic.

One way the animals gratify Pam is through merely being their silly selves. Pam has two roosters, both over thirteen years old. These two crow at night to the moon, rather than in the morning to the sun. "They're showing their age," Pam laughs, admitting that she loves them even though their clocks are off.

Then there's Coon, the cat. When Pam is out in the barn feeding and happens to be on the portable phone, Coon sits on the phone inside the house and dislodges the mouthpiece from the cradle. Coon then meows to page her until she returns to the house.

Then there's Jenny, the sandwich eating gray and white paint burro. Jenny adores bread, so every evening Pam must make her a sandwich so she can sleep the entire night undisturbed. Pam has no idea how or where Jenny got her appetite for bread, but she does know that Jenny can be very loud if denied her culinary fancy.

Then there's Duncan, the Great Pyrenees with a sweet tooth. If he doesn't get a sweet treat from Pam at night, he'll just help himself to one or two, or maybe even several pounds of candy. One evening his craving drove him to open the cupboard and eat an entire bag of candy suckers. He left the sticks on the dining room floor for Pam to clean up the next morning.

Then there's Zeena's collection of horse toys. Every evening, Zeena digs a hole in her stall and carefully places her cherished belongings, stuffed animals and balls, inside for safe keeping. Every morning, Pam empties the hole and fills it, but every night, Zeena again buries her treasures.

Anyone who believes that animals are dumb ought to visit Pam's house. The depth of communication between Pam and her group merits attention.

Zeena and Zero and Trevor are Pam's best friends. Without them, her life would be empty, humorless, and certainly boring.

Healing a Depressed Heart

Marguerite Janiszyn
Keen, New Hampshire

In 1917, Marion Garretty wrote, "To be loved by a horse, or by any animal, should fill us with awe." These words ring true for Marguerite Janiszyn. When she reflects on her turbulent adolescent years and recalls the special love of a horse named Oskar, Marguerite is filled with awe. Oskar's love saved her life.

As an adolescent, Marguerite suffered from depression. Many aspects of her young life were bewildering and chaotic. Her parent's divorce left a cloud of confusion hanging over the family. School life was just as tough. Marguerite says that she didn't have many friends. To make matters worse, she's dyslexic. Consequently, many of her classmates thought she was slow and made fun of her. Her mom, Barbara, and her dad, Mike, tried to help her, but Marguerite still had difficulty coping. She admits that she thought of suicide.

Then on Marguerite's thirteenth birthday, love and light filled her life. Her parents presented her with Oskar, a 15.3 hand chestnut Saddlebred cross. He had been at the farm where Marguerite took riding lessons, and she was quite familiar with him. In fact, she was the only person who could handle him at times. Marguerite suspects that he had been abused before he was sold to the farm. "He was head shy," she explains. "He was also antisocial with other horses, as well as with people, and he disliked men."

Marguerite's admiration for Oskar wasn't a secret. She started saving money to buy him. She even created the Oskar Fund, selling vegetables and painting and selling horse pictures to raise the funds to make her dream of owning him a reality. Her parents knew how much Oskar meant to Marguerite, so on her birthday, they surprised her by driving to the farm where Oskar waited with a big pink bow tied in his mane.

The two already shared a bond, but after Oskar became her very own horse, this bond strengthened and grew by leaps and bounds. Oskar was Marguerite's best friend. She worked at the farm caring for the other horses to help pay for his board. She spent her every free moment with him. Marguerite even lived with Oskar in his stall for a time while she lovingly nursed him back to health after he met with an accident.

He had been in a pasture with fence posts lying all around. When the horses were called in for dinner, they exuberantly responded. The horse in front of Oskar stepped on a post making it rise. Oskar took the point of the post in his chest. It was a freak accident and a serious one. Oskar needed 120 stitches to close his chest. To make things worse, an artery in his leg had also been severed. Marguerite slept in his stall and applied compresses to his leg for days and nights—for eight months! Oskar recovered, and his accident brought the two closer together.

As time went on, she and Oskar won blue ribbons in many local shows, dressage and combined training events. Marguerite gained respect among her peers because of her riding abilities, and she credits Oskar with her successes in the ring, and says, "He taught me everything I know about riding."

Now a beautiful young woman, Marguerite is an art major in college, and plans to someday teach. Her sensitive nature is soothed by painting and teaching riding to horse crazy kids. When time allows, she also trains and prepares horses for riding. Marguerite teaches, "Riding isn't about mastery over another creature. It's about the union of the two creatures."

Although her schedule is hectic, Marguerite sees Oskar as often as she can. She's certain that his special love kept her going through a horrible time in her life. "He loved me no matter what," Marguerite says.

Oskar's pure, unconditional love is indeed a reason to inspire awe in us all.

Healing through Bringing a Soul to Life

Debra Hindlemann Webster
Denver, Colorado

Hillary Webster is an active child with large gray eyes and inch-long brown hair. She was born with multiple congenital anomalies: Hillary has been tube-fed since birth; she has a breathing tube; impaired fine and gross motor control, and autistic tendencies. Hillary has massive cranial nerve damage that affects the operation of nerves in her neck and face; hence, her sensory, vocal, and eating abilities are affected. She is also deaf and has Tourette Syndrome.

Hillary has been kept alive with five life-support machines and requires 24-hour medical care. She can feel and see, but she can't smell, taste, nor hear. Although she knows some sign language, she has a major language disorder. Yet despite the challenges, her mom, Debra, points out, "Hillary is bright and strong-willed. She has been raised as a well child. She lives at home, goes to public school, and she has friends."

Always looking for ways to encourage her daughter to respond to her environment, Debra enrolled Hillary in a therapeutic riding program. Debra had read that therapeutic riding often proved beneficial. She felt that what it offered—a sense of locomotion, self-esteem and control, and bonding—were worthwhile pursuits. When Hillary turned five, she began weekly lessons.

Debra cautions, "It's difficult to specifically gauge the effect that the horses had on Hillary because she can't speak for herself or express her thoughts as others do; however, there's every reason to believe that her riding experience helped enormously."

Debra's main goal was to provide Hillary with the opportunities riding offered. The horses were available to show the students the sensation of locomotion. Debra reports, "The horses' movements beneath Hillary were as though they were her own." Hillary began to walk.

Hillary had been in traditional physical therapy since birth, so it's impossible to say which form of therapy contributed what, or which was the more influential. Yet after two years of riding, Hillary was able to walk independently—she finally understood the process.

Riding definitely helped Hillary gain a sense of control and self-esteem. At times Hillary would cry when she was first put on the horse, but when asked if she wished to get down, she refused. She insisted on continuing her lessons. Riding gave her the feeling that she was someone special; she could finally do something none of her friends knew how to do.

Hillary took lessons for six years. Debra says she looked forward to the relationship she shared with the animals. "She treasured the grooming, the saddling and unsaddling, and the feeding time. It was soothing to both Hillary and her mount." She enjoyed watching the animals for hours—mostly their lips and whiskers, especially how they moved when they ate. Perhaps it was because Hillary's facial muscles are paralyzed; perhaps it was because Hillary can't eat by mouth. Whatever the reason, she was fascinated.

Possibly the most important achievement gained from therapeutic riding was that Hillary made friends with the horses. She allowed them into her withdrawn, silent world, and they helped her to understand how to reach out and relate to others.

Hillary made significant strides during her six years of therapeutic riding. She participated in the Special Olympics and in multiple horse shows. She won several ribbons—an opportunity that field-days in public school did not offer children with multiple disabilities.

As the years have gone by and Hillary has matured, her experiences have broadened and her interests have narrowed. She focuses on those activities that she does best. Riding has become less of a priority, replaced with art, computers, and picture books.

"Even though her interests have changed, there is every reason to believe that therapeutic riding was a significant influence in her life," Debra states. "The animals encouraged my daughter to accept the challenges of movement, of increased self-confidence and self-esteem, and of increased empathy with other living beings."

Healing through Kindness

B.O.K Ranch
Los Altos Hills, California

I n a society whose members so often are inconsiderate, if not downright hostile, it stirs the spirit to know that there are in fact kind, thoughtful, generous, and considerate people. Ann Kulchin and her daughters Dede and Leslie are three such people; they founded B.O.K Ranch 11 years ago—as a family project—to help the physically, mentally, and emotionally challenged know that they can feel pride in their success and Be O.K.

Although Ann, Larry, Dede, and Leslie had been involved with horses and 4-H programs for years, B.O.K really started when Dede was working on her master's thesis in human and animal bonding. Faced with writing a thesis in special education, one evening Dede saw a television show which featured a blind man riding a horse. It struck her as incredible, and she wanted to know more about it to become involved in such challenges.

Soon afterward, the family attended a special education convention and they watched a video on therapeutic riding. Not long afterwards, Dede and Leslie became licensed therapeutic riding instructors and B.O.K opened to the public.

B.O.K has grown since its opening; it currently handles 35 students with the help of 45 volunteers and one riding instructor, Carol Studer. Although B.O.K devotes itself to helping any and all who need its services, it seems that lately it's specializing in helping autistic children.

Ann, Carol, and many happy parents have witnessed marvelous occurrences at B.O.K. According to the medical textbooks, an autistic child is tactile-sensitive and avoids touch, yet B.O.K has several autistic clients who are overcoming their tactile sensitivity. One autistic child delights in burying her face and hands in a pony's mane. Carol reports another autistic adolescent who wouldn't go near the horses when he first started to visit B.O.K. Now, three months later, he loves to brush and pet the horses. "When his mom first saw him brushing a horse," Carol says, "she was aghast."

One of the most satisfying occurrences at B.O.K happened to a little autistic girl just recently. When she first entered the program, she couldn't express her wants or desires. It was frustrating for everyone involved—especially the child. When she wished to dismount, she'd let others know by an emotional outburst; it was all she could do. But after several months at B.O.K, she learned a new and better way to communicate. Now when she wants to dismount, she says "helmet" which lets Carol know that the lesson is over. The work at the ranch which has helped to teach her to express herself has carried over into other aspects of her life, and she is developing language skills.

To the average parent saying "helmet" may not seem like much, but to the parent of an autistic child, it means the world and more, for it's an indication of remarkable progress. Ann attributes such success to magic and maintains, "Magic happens between the horses and children."

B.O.K has three star performers who cast their equine spells on the children. Two of these are Norwegian Fjord ponies, P.J. and Zeke. P.J., by the way, is named for the Kulchin's pastor, Pastor Jerry, who noticed Norwegian Fjords at a horse show.

After admiring these beautiful animals, Pastor Jerry Dummler told Ann that given their temperament, they'd make great additions to a therapeutic riding program. And sure enough, they are excellent mounts for the children. Ann refers to the Fjords as the Cadillac of the therapy horse, for they are indeed intelligent, hardy, and gentle. Both ponies get on well with the other four-legged therapist at B.O.K, Shale, a white Arab Paso Fino cross.

Keeping in step with Ann's gracious nature, B.O.K Ranch has a scholarship program. No child is denied the chance to ride and to feel self-esteem. If a doctor approves therapeutic riding for a patient, you can bet that child will be riding, even if his or her parents are unable to pay. According to Carol, "We don't turn anyone down if they can't afford it."

Dede was dumbfounded when asked, "Why does your family care?" The question was so foreign that Dede couldn't respond. After several silent moments, Dede said, "If everybody helped each other, the world would be a much different place. What I give to others comes right back to me. It's mutual giving and receiving."

Helping others is a way of life for Ann and her daughters; it's engraved on their hearts. All three women believe that animals are powerful catalysts for change, and all three women love and respect their animal kin, especially the horse. It's only natural for them to help others with and through the help of horses.

Dede summed it all up through a metaphor. Referring to the family's first horse, Cocoa, a Morgan Quarterhorse cross, she said, "He blossomed through love." B.O.K Ranch is living proof of the power of love.

Healing Through Empowering

Dr. Thomas Matola
San Jose, California

Ralph Waldo Emerson, in his essay "Heroism", wrote "The characteristic of heroism is its persistency." Dr. Tom Matola has tested and lived the truth of this statement since 1991 when he suffered a debilitating stroke which left him unable to talk and unable to use the right side of his body. Tom was angry. He felt that his body had betrayed him, and admits that he lost much of his courage because of the stroke. He went through conventional rehabilitation and he improved. However, it was only after participating in therapeutic riding that Tom found his courage again.

It wasn't easy for Tom to decide to ride. He and his wife, Roberta Johnson, a retired judge, knew of the positive effects of hippotherapy, using the horse as a therapist. Their sister-in-law, Ann Kulchan, is the founder and director of B.O.K Ranch, a therapeutic riding center located in Los Altos Hills, California. Tom and Roberta had visited B.O.K on many occasions and witnessed the progress made by children with cerebral palsy. Yet, Tom was scared of horses.

Prior to his stroke, Tom had been on a horse only once and it wasn't a great experience. The animal, an ex-racing horse, decided that they were going to go for a dip in the ocean. Tom disagreed, but she won the argument. The experience terrified Tom and left him with bitter memories. Tom was understandably resistant to the idea of riding—therapeutic or not.

Roberta and Ann, however, knew full well that the effects of Tom's stroke could be lessened with the help of horses, so they kept talking to him. It didn't take long for the talking to work. Tom soon realized that he had to ride. He understood that he wouldn't get better unless he helped himself and he yearned to improve.

Determined to progress physically, Tom told himself, "I'm going to turn this around." He began riding at B.O.K Ranch.

After a time, Ann suggested that he move to the National Center for Equine Facilitated Therapy in Woodside, California. This center was better equipped to help Tom. Barb Heine, the director, even put in a hoist to make it easier for Tom to mount his horse.

When asked whether or not riding has improved his condition, Tom responds, "Absolutely." He is talking again and his pelvic region has become stronger, and his posture has improved. Tom also has more strength in his arms. Though he isn't walking yet, he can and does stand in the saddle strengthening his legs and preparing to take his next steps. Tom has every intention of not only walking again, but of getting back into Tango competition. In fact, several years ago he won a Tango championship.

Tom has been riding Dudley at the National Center for about two years. He believes that Dudley will help him reach his goal of dancing again; he also believes that one of Dudley's greatest gifts is his energy. "Horses have a lot of energy. I can feel it." Tom adds, "It's all transferred."

Tom also believes that riding presents a chance for a person to experience a oneness with another creature. He is quick to point out that eastern religions teach that this experience is the source of spiritual enlightenment. Besides feeling a oneness or unity, Tom says that riding also teaches a person to be present in the moment. "Every moment that I am on a horse, I must feel and trust that horse," he states. "In essence, we blend our energies." After talking with Tom, a person is left with the feeling that for him riding Dudley is much more than sitting on top.

Besides helping Tom experience ancient insights into religion and philosophy, Dudley has also helped him grow psychologically. He has regained confidence in himself and in his abilities. Dudley empowers him. "If I can get on a horse, I can do anything," Tom laughs.

Tom's attitude reflects in other areas of his life. He can indeed do anything—and he does. Roberta reports that Tom's schedule keeps him out and about six to eight hours a day! He has much to keep himself busy. Tom is a writer and has published many articles in both scholarly and mainstream journals. Since the stroke still affects Tom's right hand, he taught himself to use the computer keyboard with his left hand. When he's not writing, Tom will often visit hospitals and rehabilitation centers where he helps others cope with the effects of strokes.

In an article entitled, "You Must Maintain Hope After a Stroke," Tom writes, "My mission in life is to continue as a teacher." Tom is certainly dedicated to his calling. He not only shares his knowledge and experience with others who have suffered from strokes, he inspires them and urges them to have faith and hope. Tom teaches that without hope, a person's psyche and spirit wither away. He believes these effects are as bad—if not worse—than the physical effects from an illness.

Tom teaches priceless lessons using more than words. He is a living, breathing, flesh and blood inspiration to others. Riding has opened his mind and given him countless new avenues to explore. Practicing what he preaches, Tom finished his doctoral dissertation after his stroke and received his Ph.D. in Sexology.

Courage? Persistence? Tom lives it. What's best is that he shares it with others, empowering them as he has been empowered. As the saying goes, "What goes around comes around."

Healing Through Reconciling Past and Future

Carol and Sam Studer
Mountain View, California

On August 10, 1996 Sam and Carol Studer were married in Vermont in the field of her childhood home. Given the usual humidity of a Vermont summer, both Carol and Sam were concerned that if the temperature continued to climb their outdoor wedding would be remembered as sticky and uncomfortable. But on that day, the temperature in the velvet green hills of Vermont was perfect as Carol rode down the aisle on Bun, a 14.1-hand dark brown Morgan gelding formally named Black Diamond.

Approaching 40, Bun has been a part of Carol's life since she was 14. It was only fitting that Bun serve as the reconciling link between adolescence and her future as a married woman. Bun was a pivotal figure aiding Carol in one of the most important transitions of her life. As he had walked near her during her adolescent years, so too did he walk near her as she entered her adult, married life.

When Carol was a little girl, she proclaimed to her family that when she married, she'd marry a horse. They almost believed her. Bun had been Carol's first sweetheart; she knew him long before she ever met Sam. Knowing Carol's love for Bun, her parents, Maisie and Chuck, accepted the idea of Carol riding Bun down the aisle. Carol confides that at first they thought the idea a tad risky, but after considering what Bun had always meant to her, they warmly accepted the idea.

Growing up in the small town of West Brattleboro, Vermont, there weren't that many children Carol's age around the area; consequently, Bun was Carol's best friend. Carol chuckles when she confesses that Bun probably kept her out of trouble. She spent most of her free time with him. Bun taught her how to ride, and as the years passed, she blossomed into quite an accomplished horsewoman.

She was a collegiate equestrian rider. Having majored in psychology Carol went on to work with adolescents in a psychiatric hospital. After a few years, she moved to California, became a certified riding instructor, and began working at B.O.K Ranch. At B.O.K, she exercises her talents working with horses and helping the physically, mentally, and emotionally challenged.

But California had more in store for Carol besides a new profession at B.O.K; she met the man of her dreams, her knight in shining armor, Sam. After dating for three years, they knew that they were ready to commit to one another.

When Carol discussed the idea of riding Bun down the aisle, Sam not only accepted it, he thought it great. So great that Sam rode a gray Arab, named Count Del Reno, to meet his beautiful bride near the altar. Other men might have felt threatened by Carol's love and devotion to Bun—but not Sam. In the generous spirit of true love, he showed his understanding and acceptance of her.

Carol states, "Riding Bun down the aisle was in essence saying, 'This is who I am.'" It was a symbolic statement, one that makes much sense given that her passion, profession, and pleasure in life involves and revolves around horses. Sam embraced Carol's symbolic statement and then during his vows went on to say, "I will be with you forever and love you with a passion that surpasses all understanding." Sam agreed that Bun's presence at the ceremony was necessary. Bun served as a reminder that the past is very much alive in the present.

So with the flower girl and ring bearer leading the bridal procession, the bridesmaids walking in front of Carol and Bun, and Carol's parents walking alongside, the wedding party approached the altar. Carol and Sam dismounted and exchanged their vows of love and commitment in front of witnesses, including family, friends, nature, Count Del Reno, and Bun.

Carol's and Sam's wedding was a horse lover's dream wedding with romance written all over the scene. Bun was bedecked with ribbons and flowers for the occasion; although he tried to sneak away shortly before the ceremony to roll in the mud. Luckily, Sam and the best man, Erik, read his mind and interrupted his plan.

Bun somehow knew that he had a very special duty to perform for the occasion. Having spent the night at the log cabin near Carol's parent's house, bridesmaid, Heather Harrel, woke up at five o'clock that morning. When she looked out of the window to appreciate the sunrise, Bun was waiting there staring in the window. After seeing Heather, he was satisfied that the bridal party was indeed awake and he trotted off.

At Carol and Sam's request, the preacher began the wedding ceremony by reading a passage written about the horse: "Grace is laced with muscle and strength and by gentleness confined." The words not only describe horses, but also Sam and Carol's love for each other, strong and yet gentle.

Healing A Broken Heart

Cindy and Christie Mitchell
Ontario, Canada

Cindy Mitchell of Brighton, Ontario, Canada grew up with horses, so it was natural for her to want to raise her own children in their company. Cindy wanted her children to taste "the pleasure and relaxation of an afternoon ride," and "the passion that flows in the blood of a horse lover." But Cindy didn't bargain for losing the horse and helping her daughter, Christie, deal with the loss.

At four years old, Christie knew how to ride. Sable, an eight-year-old Appaloosa, was not only Christie's trusted mount, she was Christie's best friend. Together they trained for youth classes. Christie had high hopes for the show ring; her eyes were focused on the future and the many fortunes it promised.

Cindy says that Christie's nights were spent dreaming about her next horse show and the day that Sable would be bred. Christie yearned for a filly; in her imagination, she saw the spunky, perfect filly dancing in the pasture. Cindy made plans in order to make her daughter's dream come true and chose a beautiful chestnut stallion, Silver Edition, for Sable.

Then one morning, mother and child went to the barn as they had done so many times before. Sable nickered as always, but Cindy saw she was down and that something was drastically wrong. Cindy called the vet, but he couldn't save Sable. She died of colic later that morning with her head resting in Cindy's lap.

Reflecting back to that horrible day, Cindy remembers thinking: how do you tell a little girl that she'll never see her best friend again? "It's hell explaining death to a child, especially when it's so sudden and unexpected. I didn't understand it myself."

Cindy tried to help her daughter through the grief as the months went by, but Christie's heart was broken. Sometimes she would catch Christie crying and she would try to comfort her. Yet Christie's words were always the same, "I'm missing Sable." When Christie said her prayers at night, her last words were to ask God to take special care of her little mare.

Both mother and daughter missed the companionship of horse care as well as the fun of riding. Sable's death had left a painful void in their lives, so Cindy decided it was time to get another horse. She scouted magazines, billboards, newspapers, riding schools, horse shows, and auctions. She admits, "I wrote a lot of letters pouring my heart out to complete strangers." Finding that special horse became quite a challenge.

Finally after months of searching, during a visit to a stable that had many horses for sale, Christie zoned in on a chestnut mare with a white blaze—the horse looked just like Sable. The mare was from the race track and initially Cindy wasn't excited about this prospect at all. With monumental reservations, she kept silent and still as she watched Christie introduce herself to the mare who lowered her head in greeting when the little girl stepped into her stall.

On their way home, Christie went on and on about the mare—how soft her nose was, what a pretty face she had, and how she could almost touch the sky while sitting on the mare's back. Cindy found herself asking about the mare, and a short time later, the horse was delivered to their barn.

Cindy had a feeling that the mare belonged with the family. Despite her track history, something told Cindy that the mare was the right and only choice. Christie didn't waste time in naming the horse Red, the color of her coat with the sunlight washing over it. Nor did it take long for Christie and Red to forge a bond. Red never moved when Christie mounted her, and Cindy noticed that the mare became much more calm and quiet whenever Christie was on top.

Cindy believes, "It was as if the mare had a sixth sense—this mare from the track who had a different owner for every year of her life. It was as if she were saying that I could trust her with my little girl's heart."

Cindy did trust the mare with Christie's heart, and Red healed it. Nothing could bring Sable back, but Red became a sort of substitute. Red helped Christie accept the loss of Sable.

Christie says, "Sable made me feel warm in my heart until she died, and then my heart felt all achy and sore. I thought the pain would always be with me." As time went on, Christie explains, "The hurting didn't happen as much, though I still thought a lot about Sable. Now, there's a warm place in my heart for Red."

In retrospect, Cindy understands that what she did was to teach her daughter that despite the pain and sorrow of losing a beloved friend, life goes on. Cindy didn't plan to teach Christie the lesson, but it happened. The endless cycle of birth and death and rebirth is nature's way; this way can be painful, but it is so gloriously beautiful.

Red came with an added benefit when she arrived at Christie's house, she was in foal; although, Christie didn't know it until after Red had been at the farm for a time. In April, 1996 Red gave birth to a beautiful red foal who Christie named Beautiful Heart.

Cindy easily recalls the morning that Christie met the filly. She says, "A few tears were gathered in the corners of Christie's eyes. She reached out a hand and the little filly nuzzled her curiously. Christie took a few steps closer, then threw her arms around the foal's neck. They both gently tumbled into the straw and lay there contentedly, nuzzling each other." Both human mom and horse mom watched the bonding with pleasure.

Through the concerted effort of horse and human, a little girl learned a valuable lesson about life—it's good to love, and though it hurts badly to lose someone or something that you love, it's far better to have loved. Looking back, Cindy knows that Red and her filly were the threads that stitched, mended, and reopened Christie's heart.

Healing the Self-Image

Fiona Thomas
Durham, England

Fiona Thomas was riding ponies when she was three years old. It was expected of her, given that her uncle was Master of Hounds in the Lake District of her native England. "It's cultural," Fiona notes, "as natural as breathing. The English and their horses go together like fish and chips."

When Fiona was 12 years old, she was already participating in hunting and cross-country events. One winter morning, near the windswept, craggy Scottish border, Fiona's pony, Charlie, skidded in the mud and stopped five feet from the brick wall he was supposed to clear. Fiona somersaulted in midair and crashed into the unforgiving bricks of the jump.

Luckily, she was wearing her helmet. Unluckily, she chipped a vertebra in her neck and dislocated her shoulder. She doesn't remember how she got home, but she easily recalls the terrible pain when her father tried to remove her snug riding boots.

Wearing a sling and "hideous collar" for weeks during her recovery, Fiona decided never to go near a horse again. "To begin with," she states, "being burdened with such unattractive dress at such a young age was quite an embarrassment. Secondly, I was scared to death of the animals. All my passion for them was drained from me because I was repeatedly told how lucky I was not to be paralyzed."

Fiona's psychological bumps and bruises lasted well into the next year when she and her family moved to Durham, England. Feeling out of place in the new town, Fiona embraced a new-found friend, Ellen, at school. They became close friends, but much to Fiona's dismay, Ellen was horse crazy. She dragged Fiona to a nearby stable at every opportunity.

For months Fiona kept her distance from the horses. Then one day, she was asked if she'd groom Sham, a gray gelding, half Arabian and half Connemara. She was hesitant, but peer pressure got the best of her.

Soon, Fiona was in Sham's stall nearly everyday. "I grew to trust him," she explains. "I could squeeze around him or limbo under him. Nothing I did concerned him in the least."

"I grew tired of watching others having fun with their ponies. Slowly my passion for horses was stirred and my desire to ride was awakened," she says.

Fiona remembers, "Sham kept my childhood dreams alive. He restored my passion for horses and for equestrian events. More than this, he gave me back my confidence, which is so important during the adolescent years."

That confidence stuck with Fiona who now holds a Ph.D, in Literature. Confidence was definitely needed to achieve that high level of education.

Confidence also carried Fiona through yet another near tragic accident in 1994. Only a few months after falling, spraining her neck and cracking her skull, Fiona was riding bareback.

The passion that Sham had restored is most appreciated. Fiona believes that "without passion, life is rather dull."

Though Sham is no longer with her, Fiona still rides, but she has given up following hounds. She is now quite happy in her American cowboy boots and cowboy hat, just loping along on her Quarterhorse.

Healing Hearts

The Emily Griffith Center
Larkspur, Colorado

Cradled between mountain ranges and acres of pine forests, the Emily Griffith Center is a magical place; it's a nonprofit organization offering Equine Facilitated Psychotherapy. It's home to 60 young men ages 10 to 19, 16 equine therapists, one human therapeutic riding instructor, Cindy Sharp; and a number of doctors, psychologists, cooks, and counselors.

The Rocky Mountains and the wildlife surrounding the center create a sense of tranquility, but sadly enough for many of the adolescent residents, the center is their first experience with peace. On the surface, the residents seem like typical guys, joking and laughing, but pain and sadness are buried beneath all the bravado. Most of the young men cope with learning and emotional disabilities, and some have a history of emotional, physical, and sexual abuse. In some special cases, boys are court-ordered to the Griffith Center for committing crimes.

The 16 equine therapists and Cindy are instrumental in healing, as well as in teaching alternatives to better ways of being and acting in society. Cindy specifically calls on the horses not only to heal the boys' emotional injuries, but to lay a foundation for basic skills that they'll need for the rest of their lives.

The horses heal in many ways, one of which is through acceptance. As Cindy points out, "Horses don't judge the boys. They accept them at face value." The horses don't care about a boy's past. Instead, they accept a person for who he is in the present.

The horses' acceptance of the boys is necessary for the next step in the healing process, which is providing them with companionship and camaraderie. Some of the residents have never experienced companionship in healthy ways, just as some of them have never experienced a true sense of camaraderie and the satisfying feeling that results from working with others in the spirit of fellowship. Cindy believes this facet is vital to the center's western work ethic; it's based on the belief and the practice that "the horse is a partner in work and in play." When a horse is a partner, the animal is a comrade with feelings, emotions, likes, and dislikes. For many, the horses provide their first positive experience in healthy relating.

Undoubtedly, the most powerful tool that the horses use to heal is love. For example, one resident wrote:

What made me love that horse? I was standing near him petting him one day. Face the Sun put his head down on my shoulder and rested it there, then picked up his head and licked my cheek. I was so happy that I started to cry. Face the Sun was the first animal to show that much love toward me. I said 'I love you' to Face, and gave him a big hug.

The horses are ever-ready to provide love, which is essential for healing to take place.

The equine therapists provide the acceptance, love, and companionship which dismantles the emotional barriers that most residents have constructed, making it easier for doctors, psychologists, counselors, and therapists to reach the residents.

Once they begin to heal, the human and animal therapists begin teaching alternative ways of acting by laying a foundation of basic skills, including, but not limited to, honesty, trust, and concentration. "The first lesson a resident will learn," Cindy notes, "is that a horse is honest." If something disagreeable is done to a four-legged therapist, the animal immediately lets the handler know it without overreacting. If, for instance, a horse doesn't move after being cued and a resident begins using too much force, the animal will let him know that the action isn't appreciated. This and similar scenarios directly and symbolically teach the residents that honesty is essential to any relationship.

Likewise, the horses teach trust, for often a horse can't be caught by an unknown handler. Two Mustangs originally off the range in Nevada are often called upon to show the importance of trust. Unlike the other horses at the center, the Mustangs aren't comfortable with too much human contact. Trying to avoid human encounters, the Mustangs demonstrate that they don't trust humans since they weren't born and raised with them. This and other similar scenarios are important tools presenting many opportunities to explore and to learn about trust.

Once the residents reach a certain point of expertise handling the horses, they are given riding lessons, beginning with the basics and continuing through to higher levels. At any level of instruction, however, riders must concentrate. Through riding, residents learn how to concentrate on what they're doing, whether it is balancing, reining, or roping. The lessons in concentration are then carried over to other aspects in their lives, such as school work and therapy sessions.

Through metaphors, all of the skills learned from the equine therapists are directly paralleled with behaviors that help in human relationships. Even such simple commands like "go forward" and "stop" are used to teach the residents. After all, it's important for us all to know when to go and when to stop.

Other valuable lessons the four-legged therapists teach are unconditional friendship, communication, reading body language, goal setting and achieving, and self-confidence. When asked what he learned from the horses, one resident said, "patience and how to control my anger."

The same resident shows his horse in the 4-H Club, and when asked to talk about his experiences, he did so with great enthusiasm and pride in himself and in his accomplishments. Pride is yet another lesson the equine therapists teach. For most residents, pride in one's self and in one's accomplishments hasn't come easily. Through the magic at the center, conjured up by the four-legged and two-legged therapists, a resident will likely leave with a healed heart and feelings of pride and accomplishment.

Healing Emotionally

Eric Kinchoy
Larkspur, Colorado

Eric Kinchoy had a history of family problems that caused him much anger and frustration. His mother left him in his grandmother's care when he was a baby. Eric's anger fueled his violent outbursts. When his grandmother could no longer care for him he was placed in a foster home from which he often ran away. In June, 1993, Eric Kinchoy was ordered to the Griffith Center in Larkspur, Colorado by the authorities in Hawaii.

Eric reports that he arrived at the center with a chip on his shoulder. "It was too far away from home," he explains, "and it drove my anger even more." Eric wanted to go home and he resented "living in log cabins way out in the boonies." He fought his fate for about eight months, but slowly things changed.

"The horses played a big part in my healing," Eric feels. One day in particular sticks in his mind. He met a horse who reminded him of himself. The horse was distant, aloof, and quite abusive to other horses. When Eric witnessed the horse's aggression, he nearly cried. "I saw myself," Eric states, "and I saw and felt the pain."

That equine mirror of his life was instrumental in Eric's understanding of his pain and his later actions. Eric then began to work with therapists to learn how to deal with his anger and to find appropriate ways to vent it. "Sports is a healthy outlet," Eric learned, "and so are the horses. They come to you and you know that you can love them."

With and through the continuing love and support of his four-legged and two-legged therapists, Eric left the Griffith Center in June, 1996. Finishing high school, working part-time, and taking college courses keeps Eric out of trouble, but not too busy to distract him from his goals: enlisting in the Navy, entering a profession, and continuing to learn more about life.

Physically a large and commanding young man, Eric's experiences at the Griffith Center have strengthened him inside—where strength counts the most.

Healing Through Change

Amanda Draper
Leesburg, Virginia

In the early 1990's, Amanda Draper thought she knew what she wanted from the world, and she had every intention of getting it. But then her life took an unexpected detour with the help of a feisty Morgan mare named Flower.

It all started in 1991 when authorities recorded the worst animal abuse case in the history of the state of Virginia. Thirty-two Morgans were found starving, including several pregnant mares. One of the horses, Trucker, a victim himself, escaped from the pasture and found his way to a road where he was nearly hit by a car. The occupants immediately called the Humane Society to report a loose horse on the roadway. When the authorities arrived at the location, they found a pasture full of dead and dying horses. The Equine Rescue League of Leesburg, Virginia was immediately contacted with the hope that some of the horses could be saved.

When the volunteers arrived on the site, no one could believe their eyes; disgust and horror filled them. Many animals, including Flower, were within 24 hours of death.

Flower, two years old at the time, was so weak that she couldn't stand, so the volunteers carried her to the trailer. She and the others were then taken to the rescue's farm.

Trucker had to be euthanized shortly after he and his pasture mates were moved to safety. He was beyond help; his hock had been fractured for several months. One other horse named Miracle was also lost, but all of the other horses were lovingly nursed back to health. For some animals, full recovery took years. The folks at the rescue did a fantastic job of bringing all the horses back into condition. Flower's progress and transformation were amazing.

No one at the rescue could bear the thought of letting Flower go. Everyone was concerned for her future. No one could stand the thought of her falling into the wrong hands again. Pat Rogers, the rescue's founder, decided that the mare would live out her days as the representative for the rescue on their property.

Amanda was a volunteer at the rescue for two years before she decided to focus her attention on Flower. She had a hand in the recovery of some of the other horses and decided to test her luck with Flower. The mare was scared of people and certainly wasn't going to trust a two-legged creature again. But Amanda was driven to befriend Flower.

Amanda started working with the mare ever so slowly. For weeks she did nothing but stand in the pasture coaxing Flower to come to her for grain. Little by little, the work paid off, and after five months of patient care, Flower could be quietly led, and she'd stand patiently while being brushed. Flower progressed to lunging and even wearing tack. Amanda is convinced that "As you foster horses, they come around." After one year of painstaking tender care, Flower accepted Amanda as a friend and followed her everywhere. The rescue volunteers took note of the special bond between the two.

It soon became apparent that Amanda and Flower were meant for each other, so Amanda adopted her. The folks at the rescue knew that she could be trusted with Flower's well-being. Amanda's roommate, Emily Curtis, adopted Flower's sister, Disco (from Discovery), around the same time. Emily saw that her roommate was changing, and Amanda noticed the change in herself, too.

Both Amanda and Emily left their jobs in Washington, D.C. where they worked in correspondence for the Clinton administration. They moved away from the city and into the country to be closer to the farm where Flower and Disco live. The big city life paled in comparison to the charms of a farm.

Amanda's goal of moving to California changed. Her current goal is to continue to educate others, with Flower's guidance and help, on the abuses in the horse industry. Together they travel with the rescue whenever they're needed.

Flower is well-known; she's the poster horse and the equine representative for the Equine Rescue League of Leesburg, Virginia. Besides making personal appearances, she has been in several newspapers and magazines including HorsePlay. She's a celebrity in the eastern United States. Cheryl Rogers, director of the league, credits Flower and the other Morgans with saving the organization. When Flower's rescue photo was made public, donations kept the shelter afloat and volunteers poured in to lend helping hands.

Flower certainly leads a full life these days; a life much different from her earlier one. However, she still has reminders of that life and always will. She wears the physical scars on her hip and shoulder from that horrible time before she was saved. The mare had been down in the pasture for so long, she suffered from the equine equivalent of bed sores. But scars and all, today Flower prances "like a goddess, when people are looking at her," Amanda laughs. Scads of people see her, too, and know her history. When on duty for the rescue, Flower is living proof that horses simply weren't made to be thrown away.

Flower struts her stuff when on call—and this mare can strut. She just plain shows off in front of everyone; people she would have run from before Amanda came along. Flower clearly takes her audience hostage through her natural grace and beauty. Coming from Lippitt-Morgan lines, this mare is a gorgeous Flower!

She struts for a much different audience than many of her brothers and sisters though. They went on to win big in the show ring. Disco was Reserve Champion 2-year-old in 1994 in the state of Maryland. And her uncle, Justin, or Indian's Night Hawk, was Reserve Champion gelding for the Morgan Association of the United States in 1996.

In retrospect, Amanda understands that she was a lot like Flower in that they were both "beaten up by life." Since embarking on their journey, Amanda states, "I'm a different person." In rescuing Flower, Amanda too was rescued. She found a worthy calling and her source of bliss. Before Flower came into her life, she judged herself as "a husk of a person." Amanda believes "Light now leads me." The source of this light is Flower.

Amanda is certain that Flower had a plan all along: first to recover and to gain strength, and then to find a person who would help her in her life's work. "Flower uses herself to help other animals," Amanda says.

Those who know Flower believe that she is a mare on a mission, and those who know both Amanda's and Flower's history find it difficult to say whose light burns brighter, and just who healed who.

Healing Fears

Tammy Rohn
Mesa, Arizona

Some things are just plain meant to be. This is exactly what Tammy Rohn suspected shortly after purchasing her first horse, a 21-year-old sorrel Mustang whose name is his brand number, A-4.

Tammy first met A-4 wasting away at a stable about an hour's drive from her home. He had a notorious reputation for being wild and unmanageable. He would throw anyone who climbed on top—even the most experienced rider. Tammy learned that he had been horribly mistreated, so feeling sorry for him and tired of always exercising horses that didn't belong to her, Tammy bought A-4.

That same day Tammy decided to begin his groundwork. After four days, she felt that they had reached a mutual understanding, "He wasn't going to throw me, and I wasn't going to stop spoiling him." On the fifth day, Tammy decided that it was time "to go for it." Few people would have the guts to ride a Mustang referred to as wild, but up she went. Amazingly, the two "had a pensive and quiet, yet very good first experience."

A-4 wasn't the only new addition to Tammy's life. Shortly before buying him, she opened Gecko Secretarial, a medical transcription and desktop publishing business. Anyone who has ever ventured into entrepreneurship will admit, as Tammy does, "it's rough going, extremely stressful, and mostly just frustrating."

Tammy's new business seemed to invite a fear of failure, a fear of success, a fear of inadequacy, and a fear of starving to death. In many ways, fear was her constant companion. So the 25-year-old business woman ran to her horse seeking comfort and understanding. A-4 instantly sensed her anger, fear, and frustration. It was on those days in particular that he was most responsive and gentle. "I jumped on his back and we went for hours and hours. I talked and he listened," she says.

On the surface, nothing seemed out of the ordinary. The two just looked like a horse and a rider, but what was going on at a much deeper level was most extraordinary. The notorious, wild A-4 acted like a guileless lamb. If Tammy asked him to go to the river bed and run, he'd do it without hesitation. If she wished to go ride into the hot but quiet desert for hours, well, that was okay too. And loping in circles was just as fine an idea as any other, according to A-4.

On Tammy's most stressful days, A-4 actually took care of her, turning himself on to what she calls autopilot. Knowing that she was not paying attention to riding, A-4 did the driving for her, carrying her safely and confidently. By little signals, such as snorts, sighs, and grunts, A-4 let Tammy know when she needed to become alert to something up ahead. Needless to say, their partnership flowered through their mutual and abiding trust and respect.

Tammy says A-4 has given her a deep sense of peace and contentment. "The repetitive motion of his gait seems to put me in a trance. He soothes my nerves, clears my head and allows me to get the big picture back into focus. He makes me realize that it'll be okay."

Tammy laughs and adds, "He's better than any psychiatrist. He provides me with what I need to cope with the perils of my new business. He somehow teaches me to think about nothing." Not bad behavior at all for a wild Mustang.

A-4 was going to go to auction when Tammy bought him. He had originally been owned by a rancher, then by someone living on the San Carlos reservation in northeast Arizona. Tammy shudders at the idea of what would have been A-4's fate had she not found him—slaughter. Not only has he turned out to be a soul-mate, but as a Mustang he's the living symbol of American freedom.

It seems the two were meant for each other. Tammy's mother says that A-4 looks at her with actual love in his eyes. Tammy believes her mom, but says, "It's hard to look into your horse's eyes when you're on his back."

Healing Through a Mutual Need

Kate Sinke
Ft. Collins, Colorado

A self-confessed horse lover, Kate Sinke has been involved with rescuing horses since she was two years old. Over the years, she has saved hundreds of horses from abuse and neglect. She has also been the recipient of the horse's healing power. Her love and admiration for horses, as well as her years of experience, have led her to fill needs within her community. Kate not only directs Mountain States Horse Rescue and Rehabilitation, she has also founded and directs two other programs, The Animals Crisis Assistance Program and Adoption Services for Our Animal Partners.

As a child, Kate often visited her grandfather's farm in Iowa. Every summer for years, she helped her grandfather with his horses. Some little girls fondly remember a favorite childhood doll, but Kate still remembers the Thoroughbred, March Wind, with the broken hind leg, and the pony, Silvie, who broke her hind leg when she fell through a rickety bridge. All of

Kate's favorite childhood memories revolve around her grandfather's horse rescue efforts.

Grandpa Gaines was a horse lover and spent much of his time helping horses who needed him. Kate reports that at one time, Grandpa Gaines had over 60 horses on his property. Her first horse rescue, at the age of two, took place with Grandpa Gaines. Some boys gouged out a Shetland pony's eyes. Grandpa saved the pony from the boys' cruelty. He and Kate then took the pony home to nurse her. Although the pony was permanently blinded, she stayed on the farm until she died.

As an adolescent, Kate rode the train alone from Nebraska to Iowa. To her parent's dismay, the moment school ended, she hightailed it to her Grandpa's farm. Horses were in her blood.

Although Kate was experienced at rescuing and rehabilitating horses, it wasn't until she suffered what could have been a fatal accident in 1979 that she learned that horses could heal humans too. Kate fell 60 feet from a grain elevator. She was taken to the hospital but quickly released, for she insisted that she needed to get home to her horses who were waiting for their dinner. It wasn't until days later that it became evident she had been seriously hurt.

Kate suffered amnesia from the fall. She describes the effect of the incident as creating a world "familiar around the edges," but it was basically like she had been "plopped in the middle of the twilight zone." She couldn't remember who she was, nor could she remember family and friends. However, Kate distinctly recalled that she had horses who needed her. Weeks later, she was diagnosed properly and began the necessary road to full recovery.

Kate credits her horses with her recovery, saying, "They kept me going."

Today she laughs about the experience stating, "Horses tend to run your life, and it's a good thing they do. The horses reached out and pulled me back. They led me back to my life."

One horse in particular was a tremendous help to Kate. He was a black Appaloosa rescue horse. He had been beaten and nearly starved to death. Kate knew that without her, he would die. "He needed me badly," she explains. "Nursing and caring for him kept me moving." In retrospect, Kate is certain that the horse kept her going as she searched for a way back to her old self.

Several years later, Kate experienced yet another injury. In July, 1992, she broke both bones in her left leg, snapping them in half like a stick. The doctors told her that in December, she'd get the full cast removed and replaced with a half-cast.

They also promised that in June, 1993, she could begin to learn how to walk again, but could only expect 55 percent use of her leg.

Kate, however, had no intention of waiting that long to recover. Her answer to her problem was her Quarterhorse mare, King's Mercedes. Everyday for hours on end, Kate rode Mercedes—cast and all—to strengthen the muscles and bones in her leg. She frequently stood in the saddle to condition the muscles and to work on balance. Kate and Mercedes spent hours on the trails. She was determined to recover quickly.

Kate's plan worked. The cast was removed just thirteen weeks later, and no half-cast was needed.. Her doctors were amazed—not only was her leg healed, Kate had 98 percent of its use back.

Kate believes that Mercedes was instrumental in her recovery, paying her back, so to speak, for saving her life. Mercedes became an orphan when she was four days old and Kate raised, nursed, and nurtured her into adulthood. In fact, for a while, Mercedes even lived in Kate's kitchen. Mercedes needed Kate early in her life, and later, Kate needed her.

Mercedes aided Kate's healing process, but there was yet another horse who also helped Kate during that time. In the weeks directly following the injury, Kate had a difficult time getting to the barn. All she could do was to slowly hobble, taking quite a while to reach her destination.

Misty, a gray Egyptian Arabian, came to Kate's rescue, just as Kate had rescued her from an abusive home. After seeing Kate uncomfortably shambling toward the barn, Misty met her at the bottom of the front stairs. Kate thought it odd, but she put her right arm over Misty's neck, and with the crutches tucked neatly under her left arm, she was carefully assisted to the barn.

After Kate's chores were finished, and Misty and the others were fed, the Arab mare led Kate back to the house. Every day the scenario was repeated—Misty continued to lend Kate her support until she recovered.

Despite the help Kate received from Misty, she came close to entering a nursing home during the first few weeks after the injury. Every time the doctors put a cast on her leg, it swelled or turned black. The thought of living in a nursing home terrified Kate; she was determined to heal as soon as possible.

Kate's injury set her on a course for her work at nursing homes with Mountain States Horse Rescue. She realized how horses could aid the ailing and quicken the body's natural healing process. Her work at local nursing homes is a direct consequence of her own injury.

Kate also perceived that there were yet other community needs to be filled, so she opened The Animals Crisis Assistance Center. This operation helps families and their animals in cases of abuse or neglect. Kate sadly notes that animal cruelty and human cruelty often go hand in hand. In many cases, if animals are victims of abuse, it's likely that family members are as well. The center lends assistance to women, children, and their animals who must find safe homes.

From her experiences with Mountain States Rescue and the Animals in Crisis Center, Kate found yet another community need—finding and placing pets of the terminally ill in new and loving home environments. "The terminally ill need peace of mind," Kate points out. Through finding caring homes for their beloved companions, an enormous burden is lifted from their shoulders.

Kate adds, "Everybody can benefit from the work of this adoption service." She finds that once the animals are placed, the patient finds peace and can let go.

Throughout the years Kate has rescued too many horses to count and her goodness has spilled into her community touching and warming many hearts and souls. There's an old English proverb which reads: "Show me your horse and I will tell you what you are." After seeing Kate's 28 horses, it's easy to know who she is and what's inside her: love, compassion, and concern for all her fellow creatures.

Healing Through Presence

Mountain States Horse Rescue and
Rehabilitation
Fort Collins, Colorado

The sound of miniature hoofbeats can be heard echoing through the corridors of nursing homes because of two very special women, Kate Sinke and Barb McLeod. Kate directs Mountain States Horse Rescue and Rehabilitation, a nonprofit organization located in Ft. Collins, Colorado. Barb is her friend and most enthusiastic volunteer. Although they have rescued many horses over the years, their latest acquisitions are two miniature horses, Cinnamon and Root Beer.

Cinnamon and Root Beer were donated to Mountain States Horse Rescue. When Barb and Kate first began working with them in March 1996, they were rude, unruly, and just plain unmanageable. Both women concur, "they'd kick and bite." The first thing that Barb and Kate had to do was to get these four year-old miniatures used to being handled by people. Spending a great deal of time with them helped, as did the daily braiding of their manes and tails by two girls who also volunteer at Mountain States. Once the two ponies became manageable, they were put to work.

Today, Cinnamon and Root Beer are very well mannered and groomed therapists as they make their rounds at nursing homes. Barb says, "Even though they can still be brats at home, they are on their best behavior when they're working." She adds, "Once they're out of the trailer, they behave and their attitude totally changes." Cinnamon and Root Beer both know how to step ever so gently in between the foot pedals of wheelchairs to get as close as possible to a patient. Once up close, they revel in the attention they receive being patted, kissed and hugged. They love it all.

Cinnamon and Root Beer absolutely love their jobs. They know how special their work is and the residents of the nursing homes feel their love by having their companionship for an hour or so. The effects on the residents witnessed by Barb and Kate are often nothing short of miraculous. Both women have witnessed these effects many, many times.

One man, a retired professional photographer who is being treated for his debilitating depression, was overjoyed to see Cinnamon and Root Beer. He got his camera, left his room and spent the entire time photographing the horses and the volunteers. Cinnamon and Root Beer gave him work to do, which he did gladly with the lightest of hearts.

One elderly resident broke down in tears when she saw Cinnamon and Root Beer. Her tears were tears of joy. She confided, "I thought that I'd never see a horse again." Patients who are anxious and agitated become calm and relaxed around the ponies. Patients suffering from Alzheimer's disease become interested in their surroundings and lucid again, if only for a short time.

Kate notes that the miniatures, "reach down into the mist and lift the patients up, back into reality."

One of the most touching scenes Kate witnessed involved a young woman, barely thirty. She had been admitted to the nursing center for tremors. Her shaking hands were uncontrollable, and she couldn't even lift her hand to touch the pony. Kate gently took her hand and placed it on Root Beer's muzzle. Tears of joy flowed from the woman's eyes.

People who haven't talked to their peers for ages suddenly became virtual chatterboxes with the help of Cinnamon and Root Beer.

For a time, the halls are filled with love, friendship, and plenty of laughter. The happiness and joy that Cinnamon and Root Beer bring lasts several hours, sometimes several days and more.

Barb, who works at Ft. Collins Health Center as a supervisor of medical records, laughs when she shares the story of one patient's change. One day she received a call from a woman asking what drugs had been given to her mother. Her mom was very happy, chipper and reported seeing horses in the hallways. Once Barb explained the situation, the daughter relaxed and chuckled. The ponies not only heal the residents, they also radiate healing to other family members and staff.

Everybody smiles when Cinnamon and Root Beer punch their time cards. Doctors, nurses, and administrators have all been seen carousing and laughing in the hallways and sitting rooms as the two ponies clip-clop through the hallways. When the effects of these two are seen, one can't help but smile. Both ponies cause changes in attitude, lift a person's depression and the heavy weight of loneliness. Their presence is inspiring and healing.

Like a rock thrown on a still pond, Cinnamon and Root Beer cause a ripple effect of happiness and cheerfulness. Their healing magic radiates outward touching and transforming everyone lucky enough to be in their path.

Healing With a Touch

Jill Wilkes
Loveland, Colorado

Jill Wilkes of Loveland, Colorado had a metal block about the elderly. Not particularly proud of it, Jill is, however, honest about it. She was always cautious and apprehensive around the aged until she began to accompany Kate Sinke, Barb McLeod, and the minatures, Cinnamon and Root Beer to nursing homes.

Jill holds a certificate in equine massage therapy. She volunteers some of her massage time at Mountain States Horse Rescue. Her most important patient is a Quarterhorse named Willy, who suffered a broken back during training.

One day as Jill was finishing Willy's massage, Kate asked, "How about coming to a nursing home with me today? I really do need your help." Reluctantly, Jill agreed to give Kate a hand.

But her fears soon surfaced. Jill thought, "I'm not good around old people. I didn't grow up surrounded by grandparents, so I never had much experience with the aged, let alone the aged with health problems." Stereotypes of Alzheimer's patients and the senile haunted her. Images of cold, lonely rooms filled with the smell of sickness ate at her. But she had given her word to Kate; Jill had to help.

At the nursing home, Jill remained bothered and apprehensive. She was nervous and quite uncomfortable when forced to face the psychological baggage she had carried around for years. But it couldn't be ignored or buried this time, she was in a nursing home confronting her discomfort head on. Life decided at that moment to play a trick on Jill. Kate was called away. Jill was left alone to take Cinnamon into patients' rooms by herself.

Walking down the corridor, Jill noticed that the patients were smiling. The miniature horses immediately caused everyone to light up. Excitement hummed in the hallways, and Jill felt a little better. She entered the room of an elderly woman who wanted to pet Cinnamon but couldn't. Without thinking, Jill took the woman's hand and placed it on the pony's face. At that moment, something happened. Jill realized that the woman who was unable to move was a human being—nothing more. She understood that the person laying in bed certainly wasn't someone to fear; rather, she was merely someone who needed a bit of help. As Jill watched the old woman's hand on Cinnamon's face, she felt the clouds of her fears dissipate.

As Jill had always known, touch is transforming—it's one of the reasons she decided to become a massage therapist in the first place. But it took that one brief touch for Jill to let her guard down. It was the touch of the aged woman's hand that transformed her. As the old woman rested her hand on Cinnamon, Jill saw the flowering of a human being. "She came out of herself," Jill explains, "I saw her open up."

What Jill really saw that changed her life was humanity, the human condition. The human truth is that we will all age and we will all die. The one constant is that no matter the age or stage of this process, we still need to be touched. Cinnamon was the catalyst for Jill's revelation and psychological growth.

Jill now accompanies Kate to the nursing homes whenever she can. She doesn't have to be asked, neither do her children, Cody, 12; Dustin, 10; and Ashley, 13. They all think that nursing homes can actually be sort of fun. Ashley truly enjoys working with the ponies and the patients. In fact, she wants to follow in her mother's footsteps and become a massage therapist. Ashley is an animal lover. Jill says, "She's the only kid I ever met that thinks baby ostriches are cute."

Through that one brief touch of an aged-stranger's hand, Jill saw, felt, and understood the tremendous power contained in a simple touch. She's convinced now, more than ever, that a touch can literally change lives. After all, it changed hers and her children's lives—all for the better.

Healing Through Understanding

Brita and Billy Warren
Conifer, Colorado

Many horses are acquired by Mountain States Horse Rescue service because of an ill match between horse and handler. Therefore, one of the rescue's most important duties is to place the right horse in the right home, a home that is both caring and comfortable. But what kind of horse is right for a blind boy? A blind pony, of course.

Several years ago, Kate Sinke received a call from Brita Warren who was nearly desperate. Having moved from Texas to Colorado, Brita couldn't find a therapeutic riding program for her son Billy, who is blind and is physically challenged by cerebral palsy. The therapeutic programs in Colorado near to Billy's home were not equipped to deal with the severity of his problems.

Unable to ride, Billy's condition worsened. His hamstring muscles and abductors became so tight that they pulled his hip bones out of their sockets. He had to undergo surgery to put pins in his hips to hold them in place. The operation kept him in a body cast for months.

To make matters worse, the following year, Billy had yet another surgery to remove the pins.

After he recovered from the second surgery, Brita wanted Billy riding again. She feared that without therapeutic riding his hips would again cause him painful problems. Billy needed the riding to keep his hamstring muscle from tightening and pulling on his hip bones again.

Determined to help her son, Brita was paging through the phone book one afternoon when she saw an advertisement for Mountain States Horse Rescue. She called looking for a gentle pony. Kate, who answered the telephone, responded, "I have a pony, but he's blind."

"That's okay," Brita answered, "so is my son."

Soon thereafter, Brita and Billy went to meet Stoney, an aged blue roan. Billy fell in love with Stoney. The feeling must have been mutual because Stoney followed Billy and Brita around Kate's pasture until they left. Brita says that Stoney seemed to know that Billy had special needs. Both mother and son sensed Stoney's gentle temperament and Brita knew that he was the one for her little boy.

Billy couldn't take Stoney home that day as there was much to do to prepare for him. For starters, they needed a fence and a barn. Billy was upset because he wanted Stoney with him right then.

Brita, a single foster parent with ten children in her care, began working on the fence for Stoney. She worked alone, until a local news station aired the story of Billy and Stoney the pony. Soon afterwards, several people in Brita's neighborhood volunteered to help her complete building the fence.

When Kate dropped Stoney off at Brita's house, Billy's dream came true. He has had Stoney for over two years now and their relationship says Brita is amazing. It's as if Stoney knows that he has an important job to do. When Billy's around, Stoney becomes extra careful, acting very responsible with him. When Stoney's hooves get long and need trimming, he'll sometimes trip. If Billy wants to ride, Stoney won't move. He just stands still. No amount of coaxing can get him to move.

Other people have witnessed the special bond between Billy and Stoney. Kate notes that the boy and the pony know each other through smell. She chuckles when recalling how the two just immediately clicked.

Best of all, Billy's hamstrings and abductors have stayed loose because of his riding. Stoney has improved Billy's quality of life. But, Billy can't ride everyday year round. Sometimes it's just too cold for him to go outside. Brita, Billy and Stoney really need an indoor arena, but for now it has to wait.

When Stoney arrived at Mountain States, the B branded on his hip was a bit of a mystery. Kate, Brita, and Billy now know the *B* stands for Billy.

Note:

Sadly, Billy Warren died of complications from pneumonia in June 1997. His mother plans on keeping Stoney since he was Billy's best friend. She cannot bear the thought of parting with Stoney. He looks for Billy each day. A memorial has been established in Billy's name at Mountain States Horse Rescue.

Healing Through Divine Intervention

Margo Dewkett
Windridge Therapeutic Equestrian Center
Longview, Texas

The Windridge Therapeutic Equestrian Center definitely has success written all over it. Its executive director and owner, Margo Dewkett, is the backbone of the center. Since many of the juveniles she works with have a history of physical abuse, sexual abuse or both, it isn't always easy to achieve success. But Margo can't and won't rest until she does everything she possibly can to help these young men. Her recipe for success is help and guidance; her horses help her, and God guides her.

When Margo and her husband, Bruce, opened Windridge in March, 1989, they had two students, five horses, and one teacher—Margo. Today, Windridge serves 132 students, has 12 horses, four teachers, and over 70 volunteers.

Windridge serves anyone and everyone who needs its services, and although all of Margo's students are special, she has a warm place in her heart for all the young men who are a part of Windridge's horsemanship program.

These young men are serving time for having committed crimes. After earning the privilege of attending the program through good behavior, these at-risk offenders are taught basic horsemanship skills and attend group therapy sessions.

Windridge works closely with the Gregg County Juvenile Probation Department. Deputy director of institutional services at the department, Bing Canion, says of Windridge's program, "I can't express in words how successful it has been." In fact, the horsemanship program has mainstreamed 90 percent of the juveniles it has served back into society and back into life without crime.

Margo helps each and every individual, going an extra ten miles if that's what it takes. One young man enrolled in the horsemanship program had been severely sexually abused by his father. He was scheduled to testify against his father in court—eye to eye. In order to help the youth cope with his past, Margo planned a series of exercises using one of her horses.

She took the young man out onto Windridge's pastures. She then told him to ride to various points. After reaching every set point, he had to return to Margo. After a time, she asked him to describe how he felt following her directions and riding alone. His reply was that he felt uncomfortable. He even admitted that he was a bit scared and preferred to be within her sight at all times.

Margo then explained that what happened to him during the exercise would happen again in the courtroom. His lawyer would often be away from him, addressing the judge and jury, and he would likely feel alone and scared during the trial.

Margo even had the young man's lawyer visit Windridge, in his jeans and T-shirt to aid in the youth's preparation for court. It undoubtedly helped him because the young man was able to appear in court and testify. For extra support, the youth kept a picture of his Windridge horse on the witness stand. When things got rough, he looked at the horse's photo and found the needed strength to carry on. As Margo says, "Kids who have been abused have a hard time bonding with people, but they will bond with a horse. The horse becomes the bridge back to interacting with people."

Getting the lawyer to visit Windridge and to take part in preparing this young man for court was no easy job. But Margo was determined.

As an ex-jockey, Margo is tough, determined, stubborn, and fearless. For fifteen years, she trained and worked with race horses. She was one of only three women jockeys in the South-Central Circuit of New Mexico, Oklahoma, Texas, and Louisiana during the time before women's jock rooms. She trained with the best, and she rode with the best. In order to survive and to succeed in the world of racing, a woman in that environment had to be determined and tough.

Bruce describes her as a stampede. "Imagine a stampede," Bruce says. "There are two ways of dealing with it. You can jump on a pony and try to circle the herd. Or you can just get out of the way." Laughing, he adds, "I get out of the way."

Margo's success may also have something to do with God. She attributes both her's and the center's many successes to God's guidance. Margo states that a long while back God's presence filled her heart and soul. One Sunday morning, after putting the race horses on a walker for exercise, she went into a stall and began her work.

During the glorious sunrise, God's presence filled the stall, bathing Margo in love and peace. She knew that she wasn't crazy, but she also knew that her knowledge of God wasn't what it needed to be. After just sitting for quite some time, soaking in the experience and allowing herself a good cleansing cry, she realized that she needed to learn more about God whom she'd just met. As any jockey would do, Margo called her veterinarian. "Can you tell me about God?" she asked. The vet, George, bought Margo her first Bible, and then lovingly guided her in reading the scriptures.

Not long afterwards, Margo was exercising a young Quarterhorse along the road to teach him about traffic. She saw a sign which read: "Deaf Children at Play." She stopped the horse and thought, I could teach deaf children how to ride. She went to a nearby office that worked with children suffering from cerebral palsy. The receptionist found her an article on NARHA's work with the deaf. At that point, Margo knew she had been guided by God, and that her life would and could never be the same again.

Soon afterwards, Margo changed occupations and opened Windridge to begin her life's work, helping and serving others in the spirit of loving fellowship. Margo says, "The center is God's work." She adds that her main jobs are to listen for guidance and to watch for the unveiling of the next plan.

The center is a mirror of God's spirit and what Margo has learned from His guidance. She explains that God told her to "Follow me," and this is what she asks of her students. Acceptance is the keynote. Just as God accepted Margo for who and what she was, she accepts the young men for who and what they are. Acceptance, however, always seems to blossom into a different flower. Margo laughs when she explains that God showed her who she really is as opposed to who she thought she was.

One of the most marvelous events at Windridge is when the horses show the young men who they really are versus who they thought they were. Several probation officers have told Margo of the differences they have seen in the young men who attend Windridge. When the young men enter jail, they speak about gangs and drugs. After they've spent some time with Margo and the horses, they talk about horses and whose horse is the better, bigger bruiser.

One of Margo's favorite exercises is to take the young men to a nearby creek on horseback where the water is waist deep. Most riders are ever so reluctant to cross. But Margo's quick to point out that they already have basic horsemanship skills, and that now is the time to use them. Now is the time to use their knowledge.

After crossing, the young men understand a bit more about what's inside them. Margo has seen many wiggle their fingers into the horse's mane while crossing the creek. With the help of the horses, they learn that trust is the foundation for relationships. The exercise teaches and shows trust, trust in their mounts and trust in themselves. It also teaches them to apply what they've been taught. They can then take what they've learned in the exercise and apply it in their daily activities.

The horses not only teach the boys about trust, they also teach invaluable lessons about love and care. By far one of the most important jobs the horses do is to show them that they can use their hands.

"Hands," Margo states, "are a valuable commodity. If they can use their hands, they can get a job." Margo has the young men using their hands at every opportunity. Some have been taught sign language, carpentry, mechanics, horseshoeing, and construction. Margo even has two new barn doors that testify to the young men's hands-on talent.

Margo points out that "On the track, the horses are used for monetary gains. The horses at Windridge are used for the reasons they were created. To help, to teach, to accept, and to love unconditionally." The twelve horses at Windridge teach, accept, and love. There are eight Quarterhorses, three Arabians, and one Clydesdale-Morgan cross.

Margo believes that the horses effortlessly reflect divinity and purity. She knows of the lasting changes they make in many of the young mens' lives by allowing them to taste freedom, and beauty, and nature.

As Margo looks out toward the horses dotting the landscape, a verse from Rudyard Kipling plays softly on her lips: "We be of one blood, ye and I."

Though Kipling addressed the lines to his horse, when Margo says them, they're addressed to all, ringing out over an even greater expanse than Texas.

Healing the Psyche

Lynn Vannocker
Panama City, Florida

In 1989, Lynn Vannocker was exercising a military horse at Tyndall Air Force Base in Panama City, Florida. All seemed fine as she did her circles on the huge, gray gelding, when suddenly he exploded. Lynn remembers only the searing pain in her back.

Eight days later when she woke up in the hospital, a witness told her that she had landed in a sitting position. That day, the doctor also told her that she had suffered a compression fracture in her lower vertebrae. She was so very lucky; her story could have been tragic, but, yes, she would walk again given time.

Lynn would have to wear a steel back brace for three months. After the brace was removed, she was shorter by a quarter of an inch, but her back was healed. However, Lynn's psychological state was still shattered.

Lynn visited the stable to talk to her friends and to "see the horses," but she shook in fear whenever a horse came near her. After six months of hanging around the stable, but avoiding the horses, Lynn broke down and cried for hours. She says, "I couldn't even touch what I had always loved so much." Months passed and Lynn was torn between her love and admiration for horses and her new-found fear of them.

In September of 1990, a man showed up at the stables with a scrawny, underweight, ugly Tennessee Walker. The horse was fated for a one-way trip to the slaughterhouse. "Something clicked when I saw that horse," Lynn states. She asked if she could buy him and was told, "Yes, for $200." She offered $75, and the horse was hers. Little did she know that Justin (short for Saved Just in Time) would change her life forever.

Lynn immediately noticed that Justin walked funny. "His hips dropped, and he stumbled around," Lynn explains. She called her veterinarian, and he remembered the horse. Justin had been in an accident during a cross-country event. His rider, a big man removed Justin's saddle and left the horse there on the grassy knoll to fend for himself. Justin had suffered a broken pelvis which hadn't healed properly, the vet told her. No one knew how the horse had made it, nor how he had ended up with the man who was taking him to be slaughtered.

Resolved to help the horse, Lynn led Justin to his stall. She was cautious, slow, and deliberate, keeping her hand on his neck to know where he was at all times. But now she was leading and actually touching a horse.

Shortly after bedding him down, Justin threw a fit. "He freaked and in turn so did I". After all, Lynn was in a stall with a horse who was quite upset. Her memories rushed back, and there the two stood, trembling, hyperventilating and staring at one another. "We were both so afraid of each other," Lynn laughs. "In retrospect, it must have been a hilarious sight. I was a shaky little creature, and Justin was a shaky big creature."

Lynn fought her fears knowing that if she didn't calm Justin, she stood a good chance of being injured again. "I knew that if we were to continue with our relationship, I had to do something." Calming him turned out to be Lynn's first step toward recovery.

But full recovery took time. Justin didn't trust Lynn, nor did Lynn trust Justin. For months whenever Lynn went into his stall, he trembled. And whenever Justin approached Lynn, she trembled. "I'd think, my back! Maybe Justin was thinking, my hips!"

As time went by, both Lynn and Justin relaxed and let go of their fears. Lynn often took Justin to an inlet near the ocean where he swam in warm water. After several months passed, Justin even whinnied when he saw Lynn approach. He nuzzled her when she got close to him. Lynn says, "In time, we became good friends. He'd greet me at his stall, and we learned to trust again. I could look into his eyes and know that he trusted me."

In 1993, Lynn sold Justin to a woman who paid for the expensive surgery to help him move around a bit easier. Lynn also moved onto greener pastures. She completed her certificate in equine massage therapy in Virginia and then moved to Vail, Colorado.

Today, Lynn works as a massage therapist—horses only. Many of her clients are used for therapeutic riding programs. Horses who help the handicapped need help themselves. They overcompensate for the rider's unbalanced body resulting in stiff and sore muscles for the horses. "If the horses are to continue working and helping others," Lynn notes, "they must be in good shape and free from pain." Lynn travels from state to state practicing horse massage. She even finds time to volunteer at Therapeutic Riding Centers, such as Alpin Glow in Vail.

Wherever Lynn goes, Justin's memory follows as theirs was a most special relationship. Together they became a special team. Together they healed each other, reciprocally teaching and learning how to trust again.

Healing the Mind's Eye

Terri Ullstrup
Westminster, Colorado

Terri Ullstrup found herself volunteering at The Horse Protection League in Arvada, Colorado. She didn't have horse experience, and wasn't exactly sure why she felt compelled to give up her time. She had always been attracted to horses and wondered what it would be like to be around them. Terri was instantly drawn to Saydrah who had already been under the league's protection for two years. She describes this 26-year-old gray Arabian mare as "a beautiful, gentle horse with gorgeous, soft fur, who didn't make me feel afraid at all." Terri's title soon became "Saydrah's Caretaker."

Saydrah's earlier life had been spent as a brood mare, giving birth to 15 foals in 20 years. When she could no longer foal, her owners decided slaughter was best. When the league purchased her for $100, Saydrah was suffering from starvation and hoof abscesses—luckily, the league was there to save her.

One day while grooming Saydrah, Terri remembers thinking, "She gave so much of herself to her prior owners, and the reward for her loyalty was starvation

141

and slaughter." In December 1995, after just one year as Saydrah's steward, Terri officially adopted her. "I got Saydrah to give her a good home," she recounts.

Terri's decision to adopt came only after careful consideration. She wondered if the time was right to take on the responsibility. She also had a few concerns about the expenses and time involved. Terri works full-time in surgical sales, and she shares the duties of the Colorado Jerky Company with her husband, Dave. She also has a business, Dream-Time, on a web-site. Needless to say, many responsibilities nibbled at Terri's time. Yet something inside told her to make the lifetime commitment and adopt Saydrah.

Terri's initial concerns melted during the first week. "Everything fell into place," she says. "At first, I wasn't sure if I'd have time, but I found myself making time to learn about her." What Terri really learned was that the time spent with Saydrah was time spent with herself. "The more I nurtured her," Terri explains, "the more I nurtured myself, and the more I cared for her, the more I really cared for myself. I was happier, less rushed, and more at peace with myself after being around Saydrah. It's a spiritual healing. The best thing that I ever did was get a horse. I love her so much."

Terri now knows why she adopted her. "Through spending time with Saydrah, I have come to understand that animals are a big part of my soul's purpose. I must honor and protect them because they give so much love without ever asking for anything in return. Animals are such a great resource to have in life."

Terri also believes that what Saydrah so effortlessly offers her is priceless. "Saydrah mirrors my care and concern for her right back to me. I see myself differently than ever before since Saydrah has come into my life.

She's that beautiful part of me, or my consciousness, that I now recognize. It was always there, but I never saw it, until my beautiful Saydrah reflected it back to me."

"Sometimes," Terri feels, "you have to 'go away to come home' in order to find out who you really are. In knowing my beautiful Saydrah, I feel that I have truly gone away and come home."

For this special woman, home is where the horse is.

Healing a Silent Heart

Dona Neargarder
Fletcher, Ohio

Dona Neargarder has always known that horses have special powers to weave webs of magic around their admirers. So for the last eight years, Dona has made it a point to share her miniature horses with preschool children and old folks confined to nursing homes. She believes, "Miniature horses seem to have a special rapport with the very young, the very old, and the physically and mentally impaired." She admits, "I have often taken feisty, frisky weanlings into nursing homes to see them transform into very calm, gentle creatures who quietly tiptoe up to the bedside of an elderly patient, stand perfectly still, and allow the strange person to repeatedly touch, hug, and kiss them."

Among the green pastures of Ohio, Dona breeds, shows, and nurtures her miniature treasures at Kickapoo Acres. Sometimes people just show up at the farm for a visit. This is no problem since showing off her "tiny treasures" is a source of great joy. Yet once every so often, someone will ask the forbidden question, "What are they good for?" The question grates ever so gently on

Dona's nerves, and she's forced to rattle off facts and figures, such as "One miniature horse in top condition can pull two adults and a cart for ten miles without so much as breaking a sweat."

Not so long ago, the question "What are they good for?" was definitively answered by Kickapoo's Nickelodeon, a 27 inch silver-dappled stallion. Called Nick, he answered the question once and for all time with the help of a little girl named Bobbi, who suffers from spina bifida.

A few years ago, Bobbi's grandmother, Wilma Long, asked Dona if they could visit Kickapoo Acres so that Bobbi could see the miniature horses. When they arrived, Dona saw that Bobbi was on crutches, small for her age, very quiet, and expressionless. Dona adds, "Bobbi had the biggest, brownest, and saddest eyes I had ever seen." Dona's heart ached for Bobbi as the child struggled, "determinedly" to cross the lawn to get to the barn.

Dona tried to talk with Bobbi, but Wilma explained that the little girl hadn't spoken since her beloved grandfather had died. Again, Dona's heart cringed. With tears in her eyes, Dona introduced Bobbi to all her horses. Bobbi took an instant liking to Nick. Then something truly wonderful happened.

When Dona took Nick out of his stall, Bobbi released her tight grip on the crutches and reached out with her "tiny, pink polished fingernail and touched Nick's spots, one by one, as if counting them." Dona says "Bobbi's eyes were as big as saucers as she ran her shaky hand down Nick's mane, up to his ears, and down to his velvety soft nose." All the while, Nick stood still—the perfect gentleman.

Then all at once, to Dona's utter amazement, Bobbi dropped her crutches and took Nick's lead from her hand. Leaning against the wall for support, each foot dragging, Bobbi began to lead Nick up and down the aisle way in the barn. Dona states that she "quickly searched Bobbi's grandmother's face for signs of worry, but found a look of surprised delight." Dona adds that Nick was "intuitively gentle with the quiet little girl who was acting as if she had all the strength and power in the world, but who could in reality barely stand."

Fearing Bobbi was tiring, Dona finally convinced the child that Nick had been walked enough and that it was time for him to return to his stall. When Dona reached for Nick's lead, Bobbi refused to give it back. She stared into Dona's eyes with stubborn persistence and then she pulled the lead away from her reach. Continuing to support herself with the help of the wall, Bobbi then led Nick back to his stall, unsnapped his lead, shut his door, and checked that it was latched. Dona says, "By this time, I felt privileged to be witnessing a very unique and personal bonding between my little stallion and one very special little girl."

Needless to say, Bobbi became a regular visitor at Kickapoo Acres, inspecting each new foal on the farm and following Dona to every horse show and parade. It's not a bad schedule at all for a child who has had over eleven operations. Wilma reports that Bobbi's first operation was to close her spine. Afterwards, the doctors inserted a shunt into her skull. Bobbi had surgery on her hips, and still another operation on her feet. She is a girl-wonder, for given her condition, she shouldn't be able to walk at all, but she does with the help of leg braces and crutches.

Last year, Wilma thought it would be a great idea to breed their 40 inch pony, Cindy, to one of Dona's stallions. Although a hole had to be dug so that the stallion could reach Cindy, all went well, and Bobbi is now the proud owner of a little sorrel filly named Honeysuckle.

Bobbi works with Honeysuckle every day. She supports herself on the fence with one hand and leads her filly with the other. She plans to some day show Honeysuckle on her own, and she takes riding lessons on Cindy. Recently, Bobbi asked her grandmother for a horse, as she yearns for a full-sized animal.

The girl wonder also enjoys driving, and she even won second place at the County Fair driving Cindy. She is certifiably horse crazy, but Wilma doesn't mind, since Bobbi is doing so well. She knows what the ponies mean to Bobbi. Wilma has seen her granddaughter improve and progress both emotionally and physically, and reports that since Bobbi started riding, she even has better bowel control.

Bobbi also began talking again, but only to those who are close to her, and only in gentle whispers. "It's a start," Dona states. Dona knows that Bobbi will continue to make progress, since she is a very determined and courageous little girl. Dona also feels truly blessed that Nick was able to help.

What are they good for? Dona quotes: "The outside of a horse is good for the inside of a man." She laughs adding, "but in this case, a little girl."

Black Mare

Out of darkness the horses appeared.
White horses as crests of waves
thundering ashore;
black horses as wind rushing
in charred pine forests;
yellow, gray, chestnut—
red horses as blood—
running down the neck of night
to the pumping center.
They came out of darkness.

All night their hoofs
below my window

The black mare turns.
In her eyes a galaxy of stars,
a blue crescent moon;
shells and foam, ghosts
of men from Lascaux cave.
I had known each and every one
the impaled bodies of chargers,
the Queens buried in gold.

She thunders where we
once ran on distant
wind whipped shores.
Blue crescent black mare makes light.

References

1. Stapleton, Michael. *The Illustrated Dictionary of Greek and Roman Mythology.* (New York: Hamlyn, 1978).

2. Grimal, Pierre (translated by A. R. Maxwell-Hyslo). *Dictionary of Classical Mythology.* (Oxford, England & New York: Blackwell, 1985).

3. Sigerist, Henry. *A History of Medicine: Early Greek, Hindu, and Persian Medicine.* Volume II. (London: Oxford University Press, 1961).

4. Jung, Carl. *Man and His Symbols.* (New York: Dell Publishing, 1964).

5. Cavafy. *The Horses of Achilles.* (San Francisco: Sierra Club Books, 1989).

6. Clark, LaVerne Harrell. *They Sang For Horses: The Impact of the Horse on Navajo and Apache Folklore.* (Tucson: University of Arizona Press, 1966).

7. Ewers, John. *The Horse in Blackfoot Indian Culture.* (Washington: Smithsonian Institution Press, 1955).

8. *Black Elk Speaks* as told through John G. Neihardt. (Lincoln: University of Nebraska Press, 1932).

9. Hausman, Gerald. *Meditations With Animals: A Native American Bestiary.* (Sante Fe: Bear & Company, 1986).

Bibliography

Aisenberg, Nadya: Editor. *We Animals: Poems of Our World*. (San Francisco: Sierra Club Books, 1989). Cavafy: *The Horses of Achilles* (poem on page 16).

Black Elk Speaks as told through John G. Neihardt. (University of Nebraska Press, 1932).

Bonnefoy, Yves. *Mythologies*. Volume I. (Chicago: University of Chicago Press, 1991).

Clark, LaVerne Harrell. *They Sang For Horses: The Impact of the Horse on Navajo and Apache Folklore*. (University of Arizona Press, 1966).

Ewers, John. *The Horse in Blackfoot Indian Culture*. (Washington: Smithsonian Institution Press, 1955).

Fuller, Edmund. *A Modern Abridgment of Mythology by Thomas Bullfinch*. (New York: Laurel, 1959).

Hausman, Gerald. *Meditations With Animals: A Native American Bestiary*. (Sante Fe: Bear & Company, 1986).

Jung, Carl. *Man and His Symbols*. (New York: Dell Publishing, 1964).

Majno, Guido. *The Healing Hand: Man and Wound in The Ancient World*. (Cambridge: Harvard University Press, 1975).

Margotta, Roberto. *The Story of Medicine*. (New York: Golden Press, 1968).

Stapleton, Michael. *The Illustrated Dictionary of Greek and Roman Mythology*. (New York: Hamlyn, 1978).

Sigerist, Henry. *A History of Medicine: Early Greek, Hindu, and Persian Medicine*. Volume II. (London: Oxford University Press, 1961).

Wilson, Gilbert. Anthropological Papers of The American Museum of Natural History. *The Horse and The Dog in Hidatsa Culture*. (New York: American Museum Press, 1924).